Micah's Meals

Easy, Nutritious and Tasty
Meals for Babies, Toddlers
and Beyond

Amaka Benson

Matador
9 Priory Business Park,
Wistow Road, Kibworth Beauchamp,
Leicestershire. LE8 0RX
Tel: 0116 279 2299
Email: books@troubador.co.uk
Web: www.troubador.co.uk/matador
Twitter: @matadorbooks

ISBN 978 1785899 607

British Library Cataloguing in Publication Data.
A catalogue record for this book is available from the British Library.

Printed and bound in Malta by Gutenberg Press Ltd

Matador is an imprint of Troubador Publishing Ltd

DISCLAIMER

DEDICATION

This book is dedicated to my wonderful family – my husband Yomi and our babies, Micah and Eliana – who all inspire me every day. I love you all very much.

ACKNOWLEDGEMENTS

First and foremost, I would like to thank God Almighty for His grace, guidance and blessings. Nothing happens in my life without Your Hand in it, Lord. Thank You, Lord, for the power you have given me to believe in myself and the passion to pursue my dreams.

To my wonderful husband Yomi, what can I say? You are always there when I need you. Thank you for your support and inspiration (this cookbook has been our dinnertime conversation for a very long time now), throughout the research, sampling, writing and publishing process. Thank you for always saying the right things when I am unsure or want to give up. I love you and appreciate everything that we have.

My sweet Micah and my precious Eliana, I love you both with my entire heart and soul! I thank you both now, though you will not understand for years to come. For the light and joy you have both brought into my life, I am truly blessed and forever thankful. My dear Micah, you are my big inspiration for this cookbook. You changed my life for the better and welcomed me into motherhood. Thank you for always inspiring and motivating me. Best of all, thank you for always enjoying your meals, because without your enjoyment of my food, I would not have written this cookbook. My dear Eliana – I feel like you and I wrote this book together because I was pregnant with you during the writing, sampling and publishing process. Thank you for putting up with my late nights and photographing the meals (in my third trimester). You are already such a special girl and I have no doubt you will enjoy these meals as much your big brother does.

My sincere gratitude to my family and friends. Thank you for your support and for continuing to push me to follow my passion and to fulfill my dreams.

Jess, we started this journey together and I honestly do not know how far I would have come without your help, contribution and encouragement, especially during the early days. I love you and appreciate your support.

Timi, thank you for your unwavering faith that I was meant to write a cookbook. Thank you for motivating me and giving me the push I needed to finally start writing.

MJ and Amokeye, thank you both for your valuable feedback. Your support means the world to me and I love you both.

Sandrine, before I started writing this cookbook I was clueless about food photography. Thank you for taking the time to guide me on how to take beautiful photos, for taking the pressure off me by helping me shoot and style some of the recipes. I appreciate it so much!

To my consultant nutritionist, Rosie Letts, thank you for your feedback, guidance and hard work on this cookbook.

To Davies who handled all aspects of my book's design, I want to especially acknowledge you, not only for your professionalism and attention to detail but your patience, guidance and kindness throughout the publishing process. You captured my vision perfectly and made sure I put out a cookbook I am proud of.

Last, but certainly not least, I would like to thank all my readers on Maky's Corner for your support, encouragement and referrals. Thank you all for following my journey, for reading my words, commenting on my blog, interacting on social media and for your enthusiasm, I am constantly overwhelmed by your support and encouragement. To everyone who has reached out and asked "Is the cookbook ready?", "Can we order it now?", thank you for believing in this book as much as I do. I hope your little ones love the recipes and your families enjoy Micah's Meals for many years to come.

God bless you all…x

CONTENTS

INTRODUCTION, 9

CHAPTER ONE
WHAT YOU NEED TO KNOW ABOUT WEANING YOUR BABY, 12

CHAPTER TWO
TIPS FOR WHOLESOME HOMEMADE BABY FOOD, 28

CHAPTER THREE
FUSSY EATING, 34

CHAPTER FOUR
NUTRITIONAL REQUIREMENTS, 39

CHAPTER FIVE
HEALTH AND SAFETY, 45

CHAPTER SIX
WEANING STAGE ONE (SIX MONTHS), 50

CHAPTER SEVEN
WEANING STAGE TWO (SEVEN TO NINE MONTHS), 87

CHAPTER EIGHT
WEANING STAGE THREE (TEN TO TWELVE MONTHS), 137

CHAPTER NINE
TODDLERS AND BEYOND (FROM TWELVE MONTHS UPWARDS), 177

CONVERSION GUIDE, 245

REFERENCES, 248

INDEX, 249

INTRODUCTION

I used to look at pretty jars of baby food in the store and think "I can't wait to start feeding this stuff to my child." Then, as I experienced difficulties getting pregnant, my perspective on how I wanted to raise my child began to change. I started to think about the kind of mother I wanted to be: I decided that when I finally got pregnant, I wanted to be as personally involved in every aspect of my child's life as possible. This great gift of motherhood I was so desperately hoping to receive ought to be repaid by total dedication; I wanted to do everything for my child, right down to making his first foods. I wanted to give him a happy, healthy start in life by allowing him to enjoy yummy, healthy, homemade meals, lovingly prepared from the very beginning.

I was about five months pregnant with Micah when, waiting in line at the supermarket, I looked across and again saw all the "pretty" jars of baby food. With my promise to my unborn child in mind, I bought a jar, walked across the street to an organic food store and bought the same fruits and vegetables listed in the ingredients section on the back of the jar. When I got home, I made my own baby food using the organic ingredients, then compared it to the food in the jar. The difference in taste and freshness was immense! My first time recipe was, to put it mildly, head and shoulders above the commercial competition. That was the final push. Now I was determined to do more research into making my own baby food.

Already a keen cook, I started creating recipes. By the time Micah was born, I had a range of go- to meals for him and was making all of his meals myself. I began posting recipes and step-by-step photos on my online blog, makyscorner.com, and I started to share recipes and weekly menu plans with family and friends. I am Nigerian and, as we love spicy food, it was important to me to create meals for my son that would make the transition from baby purées to family meals easier. I was adventurous with Micah's meals; I cooked meals with bold tastes and experimented with new ingredients and spices. I loved every second of it.

Making Micah's meals, my love for cooking and all the encouragement and positive feedback from loved ones and other mums inspired me to take the brave step of publishing a baby/toddler cookbook. In addition to extensively researching all things weaning and delving deeper into child nutrition, to ensure the information in this book is top-notch, I've worked with Rosie Letts, a nutritional therapist and the founder of Bump & Beyond Nutrition, a specialist nutritional consultancy that supports women through pregnancy, breastfeeding and introducing solids to their babies.

All of which has brought me, and you, here.

This book began in hope, grew in love, was perfected with extensive research and has been finalised with all the passion and zeal I know we all have for our children. It is a collection of recipes I created for my son, Micah, from his baby stage through to his toddler stage. Although he is only two years old, he is the most adventurous little foodie I know.

Toddlers can enjoy the recipes I created for his current age and kids beyond the toddler stage can enjoy the meals too. Micah now eats the same meals as the rest of my family. Dare I say he eats better than his papa and me! Many of these recipes can be adapted to feed older children and even adults. If you haven't introduced your little one to spicy food, or do not wish to do so, all you have to do is take out the portion of food for your little one before you add the spices/ingredients that are appropriate for older household members.

The recipes for the younger babies can also be enjoyed by older babies and toddlers. All you have to do is serve without puréeing. Likewise, some of the recipes for toddlers can be modified into meals that can be enjoyed by younger babies; all you have to do is purée or mash them.

I want parents and caregivers to know that you don't have to spend hours in the kitchen making yummy meals. Parents – you can work full time, run your own business, be a homemaker and with careful planning still have time to make yummy, healthy meals for your children. I understand weaning a baby or dealing with a fussy eater can be overwhelming, so this book includes over 180 easy and nutritious recipes, nutritional information, weaning advice and weekly menu plans to make cooking healthy meals easy for every parent and caregiver.

I have thoroughly enjoyed creating these recipes for my son and seeing him enjoy his meals has breathed new life into me. I hope his little sister, Eliana, and your kids love the meals as much as my Micah does and that your family can enjoy them for many years to come... x

CHAPTER ONE
WHAT YOU NEED TO KNOW ABOUT WEANING YOUR BABY

Starting Solids

Weaning Methods

Stages of Weaning

First Foods

Strategies for Introducing Solids to Your Baby

Homemade or Store Bought

Self-feeding

Drinks

WHAT YOU NEED TO KNOW ABOUT WEANING YOUR BABY

As babies grow, which they do quite quickly during the early stages, they become more active and breast milk alone will no longer be sufficient for their nutritional needs. This is where the process by which a baby slowly gets used to eating family or adult foods and relies less and less on breast milk, also known as "weaning," comes into play. A well balanced selection of solid foods in addition to their usual milk will provide the essential energy and nutrients required by your baby. While breast or formula milk provides most nutritional needs for the first year, weaning at around six months helps your baby to learn to eat, as well as developing the teeth and jaws. In addition, you are in a position to start your baby on healthy eating habits that will become beneficial to future growth.

As a first-time mother, introducing solids for your baby can be unknown territory and it can seem kind of daunting knowing what to give your child, knowing whether your child is ready and learning about the little health and safety hazards (like choking) that can be quite scary. However, when the time is right, introducing solids can be an exciting and rewarding experience for both you and your baby. At around six months, your baby is able to experience new tastes, food colours and textures, which makes weaning a wonderful sensory experience.

The World Health Organization recommends that babies be breastfed exclusively for the first six months, as this protects the digestive system and reduces the chances of infection. The UK Department of Health now recommends introducing solids at around six months, instead of their previous recommendation of four to six months. Before roughly six months, your baby's digestive system is probably not ready for solid food and does not have the necessary enzymes to digest proteins in food. Premature weaning is the greatest known cause of infant food allergies and intolerances so it is really important to make sure your baby is ready before introducing solids.

On the other hand, introducing solids later than necessary could result in your baby not having sufficient provisions of energy or the essential nutrients required for growth. With regard to the other physical requirements, your baby could lose out and not experience optimal development of motor skills gained when learning to chew and explore new tastes and textures. As such, it is important to start weaning at the right time for your baby.

Now, just as not all babies are born on their due dates, not all babies will be ready for their first tastes at six months exactly. As your baby's parent it is your job to decide whether the time is right, depending on the signs your baby exhibits. Even if a parent has done this before, things may happen differently each time because all babies are unique. Remember that it is also important to speak to your baby's GP or a nutritional therapist in making this decision. If your baby was born full term and has been exclusively breastfed, he or she will have enough iron stored to stay healthy well into the second six months of life. Babies get most of their iron stores from their mum in the last trimester of pregnancy so if your baby was premature you may need to introduce iron- rich foods before six months. In this case it is important to consult with your GP and a nutritional therapist to ensure your baby is receiving all of their nutrient requirements.

When weaning onto food, it is important to note that the quantity your baby will eat is not important at first. What is important is getting your baby used to the idea of eating and exploring the senses of taste and smell as well as developing motor skills from spoon-feeding or finger-feeding. As babies get used to eating and developing physically, the quantity eaten will also increase and gradually they will be able to eat what the whole family eats. Additionally, you should include and involve a variety of textures, flavours, aroma and appearance. Remember this is an experience as well as a nutrient exercise.

Starting Solids

Is My Baby Ready?

Every baby is an individual in its own right, so you may or may not notice some of these signs with your baby. This is true even of babies from the same family. However, it is best to follow your baby's lead and watch out for some of these signs that signal whether he or she is ready to start solid foods:

- Even if your baby is not quite ready for a high chair, he or she needs to be able to sit up and hold the head and neck up well. This allows the baby to actively take part in eating. If your baby can hold himself in the right way, his digestive organs are in the correct position to properly digest food.

- Your baby can now swallow food and no longer automatically push food out of the mouth. This is called the "extrusion reflex" or "tongue-thrust reflex" which is a safety mechanism to prevent the baby from choking before it is ready to swallow food.

- Your baby can pick food up and put it in the mouth.

- Your baby is curious, looks around and watches you and seems interested when you are eating.

- Your baby will lean forward and open her mouth when food is offered to her.

- Your baby has gained significant weight; perhaps the baby has doubled its birth weight.

- Your baby seems hungry after getting a full day's portion of milk. (This is not always a helpful sign that your baby is ready because babies grow and, as such, their appetite increases. So this could mean that you have to increase the milk feeding frequency.)

You will also need to watch your baby's reaction to the weaning process: whether or not he or she swallows the first spoonful and opens the mouth for more or whether he or she gives you a disapproving or funny facial expression. As we know, facial expressions are also not the be-all and end-all. Sometimes those funny faces could be because it is a new experience and not because they hate what you have fed them.

Weaning Methods

There are three approaches to weaning from breastmilk or formula to family food:

1) The Baby-led Weaning Method – As its name suggests, this involves allowing your baby to take the lead, by exploring solid food at his own pace and giving your baby some independence in the weaning process. With this method, you offer your baby a selection of finger foods on the high chair table and let him decide whether to eat them or not. There are no purées and no spoon-feeding is involved in baby-led weaning, but a spoon can be pre-loaded and offered to the baby so it learns to maneuver it properly. Baby-led weaning is a slower process but it's more of an educational journey where babies learn about the tastes, flavours and textures of different foods and begin to eat when they are ready. Sometimes babies will eat nothing for the first couple of months and that's OK, as milk provides the nutrients babies need during their first year. Baby-led weaning works best when babies are able to eat with you. Mealtimes become social occasions as babies like to copy. During the baby-led weaning process, your baby's motor skills will most likely develop quickly and they'll be more dexterous. The baby-led weaning method is only suitable for babies six months and older.

Some More Benefits of the Baby-led Weaning Method:

- You skip the purée stage and you can give your baby suitable bits of family meals from the very beginning.

- It encourages shared and social eating.

- It can avoid difficult transition from purées to lumps – with baby-led weaning, babies get used to chewing from the start.

2) The Spoon-led Weaning Method – This can also be described as the purée/mash weaning method where you spoon-feed your baby smooth purées that you have prepared yourself or bought from the shop. With this method, your baby progresses through the different textures (i.e. puréed, mashed and chopped foods) and ultimately your baby can start to enjoy family meals. With the spoon-led weaning method, it is much easier to introduce iron-rich foods that your baby requires at the start, foods which would otherwise be much more difficult to chew.

Some More Benefits of the Spoon-led Weaning Method:

- If your baby is ready to start weaning before six months, you could introduce some purées.

- It's easier for parents who worry about gagging and choking.

- More suited to feeding on the go as it is a little less messy than the baby-led weaning method.

3) The Combination Method – This is a mixture of both the baby-led and spoon-led methods. With Micah, I used the combination method as you can introduce puréed foods to your baby as well as finger foods right from the beginning of the weaning process. So here you are feeding your baby food with a spoon and your baby can also pick up food from the plate. With the combination weaning method you can experience double advantages in that you can feed your baby the required iron-rich puréed foods as well as allow your baby to experience the different textures and tastes of food by using its hands and actively participating in the eating experience.

*

There is no right or wrong method when it comes to weaning your baby; each method has its own advantages and whichever method you choose to wean onto food depends on how your baby takes to the whole idea of solids and also your GP's recommendations. Since I used the combination method, this book will focus on puréed foods for babies and the transition to normal family meals, as your child gets older. It also includes finger foods for babies and toddlers.

Stages of Weaning

Weaning foods should be introduced in stages, at the appropriate ages. This is just a guide and every baby is different and will develop at his or her own pace.

Age	Appropriate Food Texture
Weaning Stage One (Six months)	Your baby's food consistency should be thin and runny.
Weaning Stage Two (Seven to nine months)	Once your baby is accepting and enjoying smooth food textures, you can try moving to the next stage of weaning – the introduction of more adventurous tastes and mashed textures. At this stage, in terms of the consistency, you can introduce your baby to more variety. Food choices can be: • Puréed • Mashed • Lumpy • Minced
Weaning Stage Three (Ten to twelve months)	At this stage, your baby can pick things up with his thumb and forefinger and can transfer items from one hand to the other. Your baby also has a much better chewing motion. Your baby's food can be: • Finely chopped. • Soft cooked. • Foods that soften or dissolve in the mouth.
From twelve months upwards	Your baby is getting older and he or she should be enjoying family meals. At this stage, your baby has more teeth, a more rotary chewing movement and jaw stability and he will most likely be more comfortable using a spoon.

First Foods

It is important to remember that even though your baby may be ready for solids, breast milk or iron-fortified formula milk will still be the mainstay for the diet as almost all of your baby's calories will still come from milk. It is recommended that your baby should still enjoy breast milk or formula milk for the first year of life. In some cases, babies on solid food might desire less milk, so do not be worried if your baby takes less milk as he or she starts to explore the world of solid food. However, if your baby still wants milk, give it to him or her and try to also incorporate milk into the solid food diet. In this way, the solid food does not interfere with the absorption of the breast milk nutrients. This is why it is important to ensure that your baby has breast milk exclusively for at least the first six months of life.

You can start your baby out with soft cooked or steamed thinly puréed fruits and vegetables. You may find that you are more inclined to start your baby on fruits before vegetables, for the simple reason that fruits tend to be sweeter than vegetables. But I recommend mixing it up (giving both) so your baby won't develop a taste for sweet things. There are naturally sweet vegetables you can start your baby out with such as carrots, butternut squash and sweet potatoes.

Micah's Favourite First Foods:

- **Carrots:** These make one of the best first vegetables for babies because of their healthy nutritional benefits. Carrots are rich in beta-carotene, which is the plant form of vitamin A, and this helps improve vision and fibre intake. Carrots also contain some iron, calcium and vitamin C. They are easy for babies to digest and swallow and they are sweet so they appeal to your baby's natural preference for sweet things.

- **Apples:** These are handy in helping to alleviate stomach disorders and help your baby's digestion; rich in dietary fibres, they reduce constipation and diarrhoea. Apples also provide boron, which is essential in helping to harden the bones. Strong bones prevent osteoporosis. Apples have complex carbohydrates, which give your baby an energy boost and they are a very good substitute for sugary snacks.

- **Pears:** Pears are a good source of vitamins, minerals and antioxidants. Nutritionally, they also help your baby's overall growth and strengthen the immune system. They are also beneficial for reducing the risk of heart disorders and lowering cholesterol. Like apples, pears also help to prevent osteoporosis as they give a balanced pH and are high in calcium. Pears are a good fruit for weaning: as they are a low acid fruit. They are light and easy to digest.

- **Avocados:** These are one of the recommended fruits for babies as they are rich in unsaturated fats, essential vitamins and minerals, which aid your baby's development. Unsaturated fats are required for your baby's brain and vision development; they are also handy in helping wounds to heal faster and controlling inflammation to your baby's skin. The creamy consistency and mild taste of avocado also make them an ideal weaning fruit.

- **Butternut Squash:** These are also a great source of beta-carotene and vitamin C, which helps to improve your baby's immune system. Butternut squash is loaded with vitamin A – which is important for healthy eyesight. They are also the least allergenic food so ideal for weaning and they have a pleasing taste and texture for your baby.

- **Bananas:** These contain potassium and fibre and are high in vitamins B6, C and B2. Potassium is useful for keeping the body fluids and electrolyte balance in body cells and also helps to regulate blood pressure. Bananas are also a good source of iron which your baby requires to replenish lost iron. Bananas are also handy in protecting your baby from stomach ulcers and they can also be used in treating constipation. When starting with fruits, bananas, specifically ripe bananas, are a handy weaning food for your baby. Bananas are sweet with a smooth consistency and closely resemble the mother's milk.

- **Sweet Potatoes:** These are a nutritious vegetable, containing dietary fibre, beta-carotene, calcium, iron and vitamins A, C and E. These are slowly and easily digested by your baby. Sweet potatoes also help to maintain water balance in the body, keeping your baby hydrated and helping in his development.

- **Parsnips:** These have a sweet and nutty taste, which will appeal to your baby, and they are loaded with vitamins and essential nutrients like vitamins C and A, potassium, calcium and some proteins. They are also easy to digest and are considered a low allergenic food.

- **Beetroot:** This is a perfect first food as it's a sweet vegetable which babies take a liking to quickly. Beetroot is a good source of folic acid and is high in potassium and beta-carotene. Roast or steam it until it is super soft and then either cut into chunks for baby-led weaning or mash it.

- **Kale:** This boasts high levels of iron, vitamin C and folate and is rich in antioxidants like lutein and zeaxanthin, which protect the eye and aid in its development. These amazing leaves also provide good amounts of calcium and vitamin K, which are superb bone builders (studies show that vitamin K is needed to activate bone proteins) to help give your baby a strong skeleton. Kale should be lightly steamed and served with healthy fats such as coconut oil or butter from grass-fed cows to enhance the absorption of fat-soluble vitamins.

- **Coconuts:** These are an incredible first fruit as they contain medium chain fatty acids, principally lauric acid, which are similar to those found in human breast milk and are scarcely found anywhere else in nature! Lauric acid can boost the immune system, improve digestion and balance the blood sugar. Fresh coconut meat is an excellent addition to any smoothie or purée and it can be eaten as a finger food.

*

Once your baby has got used to single flavours, the fun really begins. You can begin to move on to more exciting options by trying out different combinations of fruits and vegetables to make really tasty recipes. Be adventurous; do not be afraid to mix up the combinations of fruits and vegetables that your palate thinks shouldn't be mixed together. Remember your baby's palate is a clean slate and she doesn't know better – give her as many different, healthy options as you can. This way she is more likely to keep eating fruits and vegetables as she grows older. It is a great habit to get into and one that should hopefully make your life easier as your child grows up.

I had a lot of fun coming up with odd combinations for Micah; sometimes I thought they were weird but he loved them. It is also important that you do not deny your baby a type of food because you yourself do not like it. Remember it is about starting your baby off on a healthy eating lifestyle.

Finally, if your baby doesn't seem to like a particular food, it's not the end of the world. Offer the food again at another time, don't rule it out completely. At times, their taste buds just need to adjust.

Strategies for Introducing Solids to Your Baby

Whichever method you use for weaning your baby, you should keep the following in mind:

Time: Timing is key with weaning. This is a major event for you and your baby, so pick the best moment – this could be when your baby is not too hungry or too full and also when your baby is happy and not cranky. For me, I found that it was better to start with one or two teaspoons after Micah had his full feeding of milk. Other mums find that offering half a feed before the solid food and half after works best though, so you will need to find what works for you. In terms of timing, it is best to begin offering foods before 12 pm, so that if your baby has any reaction to the food, you are able to see symptoms and it does not affect bedtime. Additionally, when weaning onto food, it is important to remember that it takes time and patience. Allow plenty of time for eating especially during the early stages and enjoy it. Lastly, go at your baby's pace and stop when your baby has had enough.

- **Quantity:** First breastfeed or bottle-feed your baby, then offer them one to two teaspoons of puréed food or a selection of finger foods. In the early stages, weaning is more about your baby getting used to the eating experience and less about your baby becoming full on solid foods, so let him decide when he's had enough. Gradually, you'll be able to increase the amount and variety of food your baby eats until he can eventually eat the same meals as the rest of the family, in smaller portions.

- **First spoon:** Some babies have trouble feeding off a spoon when they first begin solids. It might take a little practice for your little one to eat off a spoon without any issues. If you find yourself in such a situation, a solution is to use your finger as the first spoon. It's soft, at the right temperature and baby is familiar with it. Begin by washing your hands, and then dip your finger into your baby's food. Encourage your baby to open her mouth wide. Place a few drops of the yummy purée on baby's lips while letting her suck on the tip of your finger. Next, place your baby's food on the tip of the tongue (where there are taste buds receptive to sweetness). If this gets swallowed, or at least is not spat back at you, try placing the next drop toward the middle of baby's tongue.

If baby likes this method, try it for a few feeds and then gradually move onto a spoon.

- **Variety:** You want to give a healthy start and make your baby less likely to be a fussy eater. You want to serve food with different colours, textures and tastes; even food you probably do not have the appetite for may end up becoming your baby's favourite food. Be adventurous; do not stick to bland baby foods. However, bear in mind that during the early stages of weaning it is best to avoid very spicy seasoning.

- **Mess:** It will get messy during each meal, whether you use the spoon-led weaning method, the baby-led weaning method or the combination weaning method. Do not expect a pristine and clean environment during your baby's mealtime. Also, do not be surprised if during the early stages, most of your baby's food ends up on her face and hands. A useful hint – invest in a floor covering like a splash mat, which can be used at mealtimes.

- **Show and Tell:** Make your baby's meal time a fun experience by showing how to eat, mimicking and acting out feeding techniques and engaging your baby by talking and making fun sounds that will entertain him or her. Talking about the colours of the food and where it was grown might seem silly because you think the baby does not understand, but try it. Another way to achieve this is by eating together; it is a social environment for your baby, and your baby can watch and learn about family meals.

- **Overload:** In your excitement to introduce your child to a variety of meals, please do not give your baby different types of foods all in one day or week. The weaning process is gradual. Let your baby get used to one new food before you move to the next one, leaving at least two to three days in between. Again, this depends on your baby and your baby's doctor's recommendation. At six months, when I started weaning my son, I left two days in between solid meals. This helped me in identifying and watching out for any allergic reactions like rashes, diarrhoea or vomiting. It might also be helpful to you and your baby to feed her solids at midday so the intestinal upset can wear off by bedtime, if it is to occur. This eliminates the risk of a painful night-time for your baby.

- **Flavour:** When weaning, let your baby enjoy the natural flavours in the different foods you give to him. Avoid adding salt, sugar, stock cubes or any other seasoning to your baby's food. He doesn't need it and you do not want to overwhelm his taste buds. You might consider using organic unsalted chicken, vegetable or beef stock.

- **Colours:** Like variety, having different types of colourful foods can also be useful and your child can get quite independent picking what types of food appeals to him. In order to avoid waste, you can have small amounts of a variety of vegetables and fruits.

- **Routine (my favourite mummy tip):** As your baby becomes used to the concept of eating, it is important to set a routine so your baby knows when he or she is going to eat. The need for a routine will become evident when your baby is between the ages of six to nine months. Having a routine is not just about when the baby eats but also the aura created for your baby and your baby knowing, by what you are doing and how the room feels, that it is meal time. You want your baby to be focused and relaxed.

Homemade or Store Bought

Mama's food is always the best, even when you are no longer a baby. You are giving your baby the best start in life and it has been prepared with so much love. Here are some reasons why I chose to make my baby fresh, delicious, homemade meals.

- **Economic Value:** From an economic point of view, it is cheaper and reduces waste. Organic store-bought food is pricey when compared with how much it would cost you to buy your own ingredients and make your baby's meal. If you are feeding your baby ready-to-eat jars it is best to scoop some into a little dish and feed him from that. If you feed him directly from the jar, you won't be able to save any leftovers because you will have introduced bacteria from his mouth into the jar. You also have to throw away any baby food jars within a day or two of opening them. The great thing about homemade food is that you can make it in large batches and freeze in appropriate portions for future meals.

- **Quality Control:** When you make your baby's food fresh, you have total control over what is put into her food! When you prepare your baby's meals yourself you can avoid additives, salt and sugar that her tiny tummy simply doesn't need. Store-bought foods are made to last at least six months, if not longer, and in order for this to be achievable, the food is sterilised by heating to a very high temperature. This in turn kills many of the nutrients, vitamins and even taste you would otherwise have if the food were homemade.

- **Varied Taste and Texture:** Although store-bought food is available for different age ranges, the textures tend to be the same so your baby is not given a chance to explore new ones. You want your baby to be excited about eating as well as learning to eat with a variety of flavours, textures and colours.

When preparing your own meals, your baby is exposed to this variety, making the transition to family meals less stressful for your baby.

- **Other Benefits:** Homemade food can be useful in introducing single ingredients as store-bought food can include a mixture of ingredients with potential allergens. If baby had a reaction to a particular food, you would not be able to easily identify which ingredient was to blame. By offering homemade baby food you can ensure that potentially allergenic foods are offered one at a time and only when you are confident that your baby is ready.

Self-feeding

Once your baby can sit up and bring objects to his mouth, you can let him start the self-feeding process. This might be at six months, or more like eight or nine months, depending on your baby's development. Self-feeding is a big deal for your baby as it enables him to properly explore food with very little help from Mama. With self-feeding, your baby can use the senses of touch, taste, sight and smell to explore whatever food you put in front of him. One of the ways of doing this is through finger foods. Finger food is food that's cut up into pieces big enough for your baby to hold in his fist and still stick out of the top. Letting your baby touch and hold his food helps him to learn to chew and move food around in his mouth. Finger foods also make great snacks and you will want to offer your baby snacks in between meals as babies and children are natural grazers. Giving your baby finger foods will enable him to practise skills like passing objects from one hand to the other.

While your baby's teeth are developing, he will find it easier to chew soft foods that can be mashed easily with the gums or foods that dissolve in the mouth. Hard foods like sticks of raw fruit or vegetables can be offered as teething aids and are especially soothing to babies if the items are cold from the fridge. It is a good idea to start off with foods that your baby has enjoyed puréed during the early stages of weaning, as these foods are familiar tastes. You want to place about four pieces of finger food in front of your baby so that he doesn't feel pressured to eat everything. You also want to give your baby the best types of finger foods that offer the required nutrients. To avoid your baby choking, ensure that any food you give is soft and easy to swallow.

Examples are:

- Avocado
- Soft, cooked sweet potato pieces
- Sliced apple/pear
- Cheese
- Cucumber sticks
- Chunks of banana
- Unsulphured dried apricots
- Pieces of melon
- Plain rice cakes
- Strawberries
- Steamed broccoli
- Cooked pasta
- Butter beans
- Scrambled eggs
- Vegetables like soft, cooked carrots, squash, peas and potatoes.

*

Babies have small stomachs so, as you'll see in the menu plans, you want to give them small amounts of their set meals with some snacks.

You don't want to overload your baby so this process works. Snacks are also a good time to expose your baby to healthy eating. So instead of chocolate, ice cream or crisps, you can offer your baby delicious healthy meals like rice pudding, porridge (you don't need to add sugar or salt), fruits, steamed vegetables and fresh yoghurt.

Drinks

Not sure what is suitable for your baby or toddler? According to the UK National Health Service, here is what to give your child and when:

- **Breast milk**

This is the only food or drink babies need in the first six months of life. It should continue to be given alongside an increasingly varied diet once you introduce solid foods.

- **Formula milk**

This is usually based on cow's milk and is the only suitable alternative to breast milk in the first twelve months of your baby's life.

- **Cow's milk**

Cow's milk doesn't contain enough iron or other nutrients to meet young babies' needs. That's why it shouldn't be given as a drink to babies until they are twelve months old. Whole milk should be given to children until they are two years old,

as they need the extra energy and vitamins it contains. Semi-skimmed milk can be introduced once your child is two years old, as long as they're a good eater and they have a varied diet. Skimmed and 1% milk aren't suitable for children under five as they don't contain enough calories. Lower fat milks can be used in cooking from the age of one, though.

- **Non-cow's milk formula**

Goat's milk formula is available and produced to the same nutritional standards as cow's milk formula. It isn't suitable for babies with a cow's milk protein allergy and shouldn't be given to these babies unless recommended by a health professional. You should also only give your baby soya formula if a health professional advises you to.

- **Water**

Fully breastfed babies don't need any water until they've started eating solid foods. Before your baby is six months, they will be getting all the required hydration from breast milk or baby formula. Giving your baby water too soon could affect the body's ability to absorb the nutrients in the breast milk or formula and it can also cause the belly to feel full. Additionally, it can cause water intoxication in your baby where the electrolytes, like sodium, in the bloodstream become diluted, limiting normal bodily functions.

Bottle-fed babies may need some extra water in hot weather. For babies under six months, use water from the mains tap in the kitchen. You will need to boil then cool the tap water as it's not sterile straight from the tap.

Bottled water isn't recommended for making up formula feeds as it may contain too much salt (sodium) or sulphates. Like tap water, bottled water isn't sterile, so it will need to be boiled before you use it to prepare a feed. Remember to let the feed cool before you give it to your baby.

In giving your baby water, you want to introduce cups of water rather than giving water through a bottle. This is especially important if you're bottle-feeding your baby. This is so that your baby is able to break the habit of sucking from bottles with teats. You can start by using a cup with a removable valve and then start using an open cup or a free-flow cup without a valve. These will help your baby learn to sip rather than suck and this is better for your baby's teeth and speech development.

- **Unpasteurised milk**

Young children shouldn't be given unpasteurised milk because of the higher risk of food poisoning.

- **Goat and sheep's milk**

These aren't suitable as drinks for babies under one as, like cow's milk, they don't contain enough iron or other nutrients that babies this age need.

As long as they're pasteurised, they can be used once your baby is one year old.

- **Soya drinks and other milk alternatives**

You can give your child unsweetened calcium-fortified milk alternatives, such as soya, almond and oat drinks, from the age of one as part of a healthy balanced diet. Children under five shouldn't have rice drinks as they may contain unsafe levels of arsenic. Arsenic is found naturally in the environment and can find its way into our food and water. Rice tends to take up more arsenic than other grains.

Don't worry if your child has already had rice drinks. There's no immediate risk and there are unlikely to be any long-term harmful effects. But to avoid the possibility of the child taking in any more arsenic, it's best to switch to a different kind of milk.

If your child has an allergy or intolerance to milk, talk to your health visitor or GP. They can advise you on suitable milk alternatives.

- **Fruit juices and smoothies**

Fruit juices, such as orange, are a good source of vitamin C. However, they also contain natural sugars and acids, which can cause tooth decay.

Babies under six months old shouldn't be given

fruit juices. Diluted fruit juice (one part juice to ten parts water) can be given to children with their meals after six months. Giving fruit juice at mealtimes (rather than between) helps reduce the risk of tooth decay.

From age five, it's OK to give your child undiluted fruit juices or smoothies, but stick to no more than one glass (about 150 ml) a day served with a meal.

- **Squashes, flavoured milk, 'fruit' or 'juice' drinks and fizzy drinks**

These are not suitable for young babies. These drinks contain sugar and can cause tooth decay, even when diluted.

For older babies and toddlers, these drinks can lead to poor appetite, poor weight control and, in toddlers, diarrhoea. Even drinks that have artificial sweeteners can encourage children to develop a sweet tooth.

Fizzy drinks are acidic and can damage tooth enamel so they shouldn't be given to babies and toddlers.

Diet or reduced-sugar drinks aren't recommended for babies and toddlers.

- **Hot drinks**

Tea and coffee aren't suitable for babies or young children. They can reduce the amount of iron absorbed from food, especially if given with meals. If sugar is added, this can lead to tooth decay.

CHAPTER TWO

TIPS FOR WHOLESOME HOMEMADE BABY FOOD

Weaning Essentials

Kitchen Essentials

Storing, Freezing, Thawing and Heating Your Baby's Food

Menu Planning

TIPS FOR WHOLESOME HOMEMADE BABY FOOD

Weaning Essentials

1. High chair: You want a high chair as opposed to a booster seat when you start weaning your child. When feeding, your baby should be sitting upright and should be well supported. The chair also has to be soft and comfortable for your baby's bottom and back. It is also essential that the high chair has safety straps so that your baby is secure. When your baby is older, then you can consider booster chairs. For your own convenience, you may also consider a high chair that is easy to clean and has very few gaps where food can be trapped.

2. Splash or mess mat: This can be placed on the table or under your baby's high chair at meal times to catch any food that doesn't make it into your baby's mouth. You want a mat that is easy to clean and wipe down after your baby's mealtime. If you want to save money you can use a cut-up shower curtain.

3. Large bib: This is very important to prevent food getting on your baby's clothes. There are a variety of bibs available that cover as much of your baby as possible during meal times. You can get full-sleeved bibs that cover the clothing. As your baby gets older you can also buy the plastic bibs that catch food dropped at the bottom, like pelican bibs. Disposable bibs are ideal when you are on the go.

4. Trainer cups: When you start weaning your baby on to solids, you can offer water with the meal. At six months, you want to give your baby water from a cup rather than a bottle. There are a variety of cups, from cups with a valve, cups without so that the drink is free-flowing, cups with straws and just a simple cup with two handles. As mentioned earlier, a free-flowing cup is better for your baby's teeth.

5. Plastic bowls: You want bowls and plates shallow and wide enough for your baby to pick up his food. To prevent your baby from throwing the plate or bowl of food off the tray, you can invest in the bowls with a suction base. At the start your baby will not be able to pull the bowl off the tray, but he may learn to, so be careful. Divided plates are also handy during the weaning stage in dividing the different foods you offer to your baby. With divided plates, you are letting your baby be independent in picking the foods from the different sections.

1. **Baby plastic spoon free from BPA:** You need soft plastic spoons whether you're using the spoon-led method or the baby-led method. You want a spoon that is gentle on your baby's gums and comfortable enough for your baby to grip on to while eating.

2. **Cleaning products:** During mealtimes, baby wipes will come in handy to clean up any mess quickly. After mealtimes, antibacterial sprays can be used to disinfect your baby feeding area.

3. **Feeding on the go:** When you are out of the house, the weaning process continues. Plastic bowls with secure lids can be used to store food and snacks prepared by you. Table mats can also come in handy if your baby drops food or if she decide to pick up food or a snack from the table. This way you don't have to worry about whatever bacteria are on the table.

Kitchen Essentials

Having the essential equipment in the kitchen makes the weaning process much easier for you. You do not require a lot of things, and most of the cooking utensils you'll probably already have in your kitchen. For me, the kitchen essentials are:

- **Saucepans:** t's good to have different sizes depending on the quantity of food you intend to make for your baby. Also, a non-stick pan is better to avoid food residue sticking to the bottom of the pan and makes it much easier to clean. You also want a pan with a lid, so that your food doesn't lose nutrients when being cooked. This is especially important with vegetables.

- **Peeler:** This is the alternative to a knife when peeling your baby's vegetables.

- **Chopping boards:** You can get three of these in different colours: one for the fruits and vegetables, and the others for meat and fish.

- **Food steamer or a steaming basket:** This is vital during the weaning process. When cooking with a steamer, you are preserving the flavour and nutrients in your baby's food. There are multi-layer steamers so that you can cook different foods at the same time.

- **Blender or food processor:** This is what is required to purée your baby's food during the weaning process. You do not need both; either one will do the job fine. You can also get hand blenders if you are making a small portion of food.

- **Food strainer/sieve:** This is handy in draining any unwanted cooking liquid from vegetables or fruits. It can also be used to remove skins from certain types of food like peas.

- **Weaning recipe books:** Weaning recipe books, like this one, offer you a starting place when trying to work out what to cook for your baby. Once you have prepared a few of my recipes, you can start to experiment with other ingredients to try with your baby.

Storing, Freezing, Thawing and Heating Your Baby's Food

When you start weaning your baby, it is essential that food, whether homemade or store bought, is stored properly and not for longer than necessary, to avoid any bacteria and food poisoning. With store-bought food, it is likely that the storage and freezing guidelines as well as the expiry date will be written on the packaging. In this case, it is straightforward. With homemade food, you should endeavour to store your baby's food in the most sanitary way. You can store your baby's food in the fridge for approximately twenty-four hours. Around this time, the food still remains fresh. In terms of freezing, you can freeze your baby food for one to two months. Plain fruit and vegetable purées can be stored for longer in the fridge and freezer, forty-eight hours in the fridge and up to six months in the freezer. When storing your baby's food, it is important to store in single servings so that when thawed, the food is enough to satisfy your baby without you

needing to throw out too much – this will come with time, as you understand your baby's eating habits. It is also more hygienic.

You can store your baby's food in the fridge or freezer, using the following:

- Mini single-serving containers with a lid.
- Ice cube trays placed in an airtight container or suitable freezer bag.
- Storage bags.
- Storage containers.

With all of these options, remember to label the lid or bag with its contents and the date the food is being stored.

Thawing Your Baby's Frozen Food

You should ensure that your baby's food has defrosted fully before you serve it to him. In any case, defrosted food should be served to your baby within forty-eight hours and you must never refreeze food that has been defrosted.

One of the ways to defrost your baby's food is by placing it in the fridge for a few hours, preferably overnight. This way of defrosting food works when you know what you intend to feed your baby and you have a weekly menu plan.

If, for whatever reason, the first option does not work for you, you can place the food container or bag in warm water, changing the water as required. With this option, you don't have to serve your baby's food immediately. Once defrosted, you can place it in the fridge until required but not for more than forty-eight hours. However, if you wanted to serve your baby's meal immediately and reduce the defrosting waiting time, you can use the microwave "defrost" setting, stirring the food until fully defrosted.

Reheating Baby's Food

When reheating baby food, make sure it's piping hot throughout. You should not serve your baby hot food – let it cool down first. Dab a tiny bit of food on the inside of your wrist or back of your hand to see if it's a comfortable temperature before giving it to him.

Personally, I have never used a microwave to reheat Micah's food but I understand that a lot of parents love the convenience for thawing and heating baby food. Whether or not you use the microwave is a decision only you can make.

To heat the baby food in the microwave, always transfer the amount of food you will be heating to a microwave-safe container. Heat the food in thirty second increments, stirring and testing the temperature after each heating. When the food

has reached the desired temperature, stir it one final time to avoid hot spots that can burn baby's mouth.

When heating baby food on the stove top, use a smaller saucepan. Gently heat the food using a low setting to ensure that you do not burn it.

Do not store leftover food from a container that your baby has been eating from because you will have introduced bacteria from his mouth into the jar.

Don't reheat your baby's food more than once.

Menu Planning

I am a big fan of weekly menu planning for my son. Food for babies and toddlers can become repetitive if you do not have a weekly menu plan. For example, if your son enjoys rice, you can fall into the habit of giving him rice every other day. Menu planning for your child promotes healthy eating; because meals are planned you usually end up with a more balanced, nutritious diet. It also saves you time and money. And, for busy parents, you know exactly what your child is eating even when you are away. Another benefit of weekly menu planning is you know exactly which ingredients you need to buy at the store.

Some other tips:
• Consider what ingredients you already have. What can you do with them? This reduces waste.
• Use a menu template – this book includes menu plans for the different stages of weaning. You can follow them or use them as a guide. It helps make the planning more efficient and less time consuming.
• I always have fruits and vegetables for the week so my son is constantly trying new fruits and vegetables.
• My son always has poultry, red meat and fish weekly but I introduce variety, so if he has salmon this week, next week he will have halibut etc.
• He always has water with every meal.
• I spend about fifteen minutes every week coming up with a new menu; this includes leftovers from the previous week and new meals for him to try out.

The weekly menu plans in this book are the plans I used for Micah. These plans are intended as a guide only and will depend on many factors including your baby's weight and appetite. You can adapt the menus to suit your little one. As always, speak to your child's GP or healthcare provider.

CHAPTER THREE

FUSSY EATING

FUSSY EATING

Truth is, it is normal for children to be fussy eaters. That is, they often do not like the shape, colour, taste or texture of particular foods. It is also normal for children to like something one day but dislike it the next day, or eat more or less from day to day.

Fussy eating is part of a child's development. Frequently, babies that are good eaters then become picky when they enter toddlerhood. It's a way of exploring their environment and, as they get older, asserting their independence. In addition, children's appetites are affected by their growth cycles.

If your child is healthy and has enough energy to play, learn and explore, he is probably eating enough. However, if you are concerned about your child's eating habits please speak to their GP or a nutritional therapist. I have included some ideas that might help if you have fussy eaters in the family:

Be Patient with New Foods

Babies have heightened senses so they often touch or smell new foods, and might even put bits in their mouths and then take them back out again. You need to keep reintroducing foods, as your child might need repeated exposure before he takes the first bite. Encourage your child by talking about a food's colour, shape, aroma and texture – avoiding talking about whether the food tastes good. Another useful tip is to serve new foods along with your child's favourite food; it will encourage him to try it.

Be Your Child's Food Role Model

Remember that your child learns by example. If you want to see a change in her, you must be that change. If you model a non-fussy relationship with food yourself and eat a variety of fruits and vegetables, your child is more likely to follow suit.

Be Creative and Make It Fun!

Try serving vegetables and fruits with your little one's favourite dips. Cut foods into various shapes with cookie cutters. Serve a variety of different coloured foods. Offer breakfast foods for dinner. Pancakes for dinner, anyone?

Don't Offer Dessert as a Reward or Withhold it as a Threat

Withholding dessert sends the message that dessert is the best food, which might only increase your child's desire for sweets. You might select one or two nights a week as dessert nights, and skip dessert the rest of the week. I personally like to serve healthy options as dessert – fruits, yoghurts, etc.

Minimise Distractions

Eat away from distractions such as televisions, pets, games and toys – this will help your child focus on eating. Keep in mind that television advertising might also encourage your child to desire sugary or less nutritious foods.

Respect Your Child's Appetite

If your child is not hungry, do not force a meal or snack. Likewise, do not bribe or force your child to eat certain foods or give him a 'clean plate' incentive. This might only ignite or reinforce a power struggle over food. In addition, your child might come to associate mealtime with anxiety and frustration or become less sensitive to his own hunger and fullness cues.

Support your child's independence when it comes to food. Serve small portions to avoid overwhelming him and let your child decide how much he want to eat. It also gives him the opportunity to independently ask for more.

Establish a Mealtime Schedule

Feeding babies on demand makes sense but it doesn't work for older children. Work out a daily feeding routine that fits around your child's daytime sleep pattern. This should include three meals and two nutritious snacks, spaced throughout the day. Serve meals and snacks at about the same times every day to help your child regulate her hunger levels and learn she has to eat enough at mealtimes.

Try to avoid giving your child a lot of milk or juice in the hour before a meal as it will fill him up and might decrease his appetite for food. If he is thirsty, give him a drink of water instead.

Ask other members of your family, your child minder or nursery staff to follow your approach and routine.

Get Your Child Involved in the Process

At the grocery store, ask your child to help you select fruits, vegetables and other healthy foods. Children love helping out, so at home, get them involved. Encourage your child to help you rinse veggies, stir batter or set the table from an early age. f Micah is around when I'm making his meals I always try to make him feel like part of this process, then the plate of food in front of him will become a lot more appealing because he was involved in making it. Micah always says, "Mama, I made this!"

Don't Be a Short-order Cook

Preparing another meal for your child after he rejects the original meal might promote picky eating. Encourage your child to stay at the table for the designated mealtime even if he doesn't eat. Keep serving your child healthy choices until they become familiar and preferred foods.

Avoid Keeping Your Child on a Separate Meal for Too Long

The ultimate goal of weaning is getting your baby to eventually eat the same foods as the rest of the family. By the age of one, your child should be able to eat meals with the family. As your baby gets older, avoid sticking to just bland puréed food. Get your child's palette used to a range of flavours and texture so he is able to transition to family meals easier.

Make Mealtime a Positive Experience

It is crucial to make mealtimes as enjoyable and relaxed as possible. If you make mealtime a stressful time, your child is going to feed off your energy, and that's unlikely to contribute to good eating habits.

In addition, try to eat meals together as a family when possible.

Keep Mealtimes Short for Active Children

Some children are very active. They seem to be picky because they don't like sitting for too long. You can:

- Set your child's meal out before she sits down.

- Keep mealtimes short – fifteen minutes or less.

- During snack time you can put healthy foods, such as a bowl of strawberries or bananas, where your child can reach them so when he gets hungry he can easily get to foods.

Do Not Label Your Child a Fussy Eater

If your child is fussing about food, ignore it as much as you can. Giving fussy eating lots of attention can sometimes encourage children to keep behaving this way.

Finally, remember that your child's eating habits probably won't change overnight – but the small steps you take each day can help promote a lifetime of healthy eating.

CHAPTER FOUR

NUTRITIONAL REQUIREMENTS

NUTRITIONAL REQUIREMENTS

It is important for children to eat healthily to make sure they are getting all the energy and nutrients they need to grow and develop properly. Your baby requires a variety of food from the following:

Fruits and Vegetables

Fruits and vegetables are important and enjoyable ingredients of any child's diet. They provide your baby with much-needed vitamins, minerals and fibre. Even if your child rejects their fruits and vegetables, don't give up. Continue to offer a variety of small amounts of fruits and vegetables everyday. Remember, any amount is better than none. I have also included fun and hidden ways to get your toddler to eat more fruits and vegetables. Offering a variety of colours including red, dark green, yellow, blue, purple, white and orange not only provides eye candy for children but also ensures a broad range of phytonutrients. As your baby grows up, he will have fun filling up your shopping basket with a spectrum of colourful vegetables and fruits that will create a rainbow on their plates.

Carbohydrates

Carbohydrates are an infant's main fuel source and are essential for proper growth and development. Offering your infant healthy, nutrient-dense carbohydrates will help optimise his growth and help maintain a healthy body weight.

The two major forms of carbohydrates are:

- **Simple carbohydrates** (or simple sugars): These include fructose, glucose, and lactose, which are found in nutritious whole fruits.

- **Complex carbohydrates** (or starches): Found in foods such as starchy vegetables, grains, rice, breads and cereals.

Eating too many simple carbohydrates can be damaging for blood sugar control so it is important to introduce your baby to a variety of complex carbohydrates. Refined carbohydrates such as white rice, white bread and white pasta have been stripped of their supportive nutrients (fibre, vitamins and minerals) so it is always preferable to consume grains in their whole, unrefined form.

Good Source of Carbohydrates for Your Baby Include:

Wholegrain cereals, brown rice, wholegrain breads, fruits and vegetables

Protein

Protein plays a very important part in your baby's growth and development. The human body needs twenty-two amino acids, but is only able to make thirteen of them. The other nine must come from food and are known as 'essential amino acids.'

Complete proteins (also known as whole proteins) contain all nine essential amino acids.

Incomplete proteins contain some but not all of these essential amino acids.

Good sources of protein for your baby include:

The following are all sources of complete protein; meat (particularly beef), poultry, quinoa, soy, eggs, dairy products, fish, buckwheat.

Other sources of protein, which need to be combined in order to provide the full complement of amino acids, are; lentils, beans, chickpeas, bulgar, oat, cornmeal, rice, wheat, pasta, nuts and seeds.

Fats

During infancy, fatty foods are a good thing. Essential fatty acids, or EFAs, are types of fat that are essential in the diet because they can't be produced by the body. These fats help build cells, regulate the nervous system, strengthen the cardiovascular system, build immunity and help the body absorb nutrients. EFAs are also vital for healthy brain function and vision.

Essential fatty acids include omega-6 (linoleic acid) and omega-3 (linolenic acid). Omega-6 fats contribute to skin and hair growth, bone health, brain function and metabolism. Omega-6 fats are found in most cooking oils. Because these oils are commonly used in cooked and processed foods, including sautéed foods, stir-fried dishes and baked goods, most babies and toddlers get more than enough omega-6 fats in their regular diets. Omega-3 fats are necessary for brain development and the development of the retina, especially during infancy and early childhood. Omega-3 fats are not as prevalent in most people's diets as other fats are, so you may need to make special effort to ensure your toddler gets enough.

Good sources of omega-3 fats for your baby include:

Tuna, mackerel, salmon, sardines and other fish, flaxseed, tofu and eggs or milk fortified with omega-3 fats. If your toddler is still breastfeeding, breast milk is also an excellent source of omega-3 fats as long as you consume sufficient amounts in your diet.

Vitamins and Minerals

Vitamin A

Vitamin A plays an important role in vision and bone growth and helps protect the body from infections. Vitamin A also promotes the health and growth of cells and tissues in the body, particularly those in the hair, nails, and skin.

Good sources of vitamin A for your baby include:

Dairy products, liver, salmon, herring, eggs, dried apricots, carrots, sweet potatoes, swede, mango, spinach, butternut squash, apricots, broccoli, tomatoes and papaya.

Vitamin B Complex

B complex vitamins are a group of nutrients that work together to help your body convert protein, carbohydrates and fat into energy. Babies need B vitamins to metabolise their milk or formula properly. The B vitamins present in fruits and vegetables are Vitamin B1, B5 and B6. Vitamin B1 can be found in spinach and it is essential for breaking down and releasing the energy contained in your baby's food. It is also good for keeping your baby's nerves and muscles healthy and functioning. Like B1, B5 also helps your baby's body to release the energy from foods.

Vitamin B6 helps your baby's body to use and store energy from proteins and carbohydrates in their food and it helps to form haemoglobin present in the red blood cells, required by your baby to move oxygen around the body.

Good sources of vitamin B complex for your baby include:

Wholegrain cereals, meat, banana, spinach, asparagus, broccoli, avocado, dairy produce, eggs and sardines.

Vitamin C

Vitamin C is important for your baby's general health and immune system and this vitamin is also essential for the prevention of scurvy. It also helps the body absorb iron from food sources. It is important to bear in mind that cooking some vegetables can lead to losses of vitamin C and so you will need to use a minimum amount of water when cooking vegetables or alternatively steam them.

Good sources of vitamin C for your baby include:

Blackcurrants, oranges, kiwi fruits, peppers, strawberries, broccoli, tomatoes, papaya, spinach, kale and cabbage.

Vitamin D

We all want our babies to grow with good, strong and healthy bones but did you know that vitamin D is as vital as calcium for proper bone formation? Vitamin D is the sunshine vitamin and many of us, particularly those living in northern latitudes, are deficient. Rickets, a condition that affects the development of bones in children, is becoming more and more prevalent and the primary cause is vitamin D deficiency. People with dark skin absorb less vitamin D than people with light skin, so dark-skinned people living in northern latitudes are particularly at risk. Please bear in mind that you must keep your children's skin safe in the sun and you should not risk your baby getting sunburnt. It is likely that during your pregnancy, you would have been advised to take vitamin D supplements for you and your baby. If this was the case, your baby would have been born with enough stores of vitamin D for the first few months of his or her life.

All babies and young children aged six months to five years should take a daily supplement containing vitamin D, in the form of vitamin drops.

Good sources of vitamin D for your baby include:

Oily fish and eggs.

Vitamin E

Vitamin E boosts the immune system and helps the body fight germs. Vitamin E also keeps blood vessels wide enough for blood to flow freely and it helps the cells of the body work together to perform many important functions. Because children are growing new bone all the time it is important that they get a steady supply of vitamin E to support healthy growth.

Good sources of vitamin E for your baby include:

Sunflower seeds, almonds, spinach, Swiss chard, avocado, asparagus, kiwi fruit, broccoli and mango.

Calcium

Calcium is vital for building strong, healthy bones and teeth, promoting nerve and muscle function, helping blood clot and activating enzymes to convert food into energy.

Good sources of calcium for your baby include:

Milk, soy milk, cheese, all green leafy vegetables, lentils, sardines, broccoli, okra, salmon, raisins, swede, oranges, eggs and tofu.

Iron

Our bodies need iron to make haemoglobin, the protein which carries oxygen through our blood. For both formula-fed and breastfed healthy full-term infants, iron stores are well maintained up to and beyond six months. By six months, your baby's natural store of iron starts to reduce and by eight to twelve months your baby may not necessarily be getting all the iron required from just breast milk or baby formula. A lack of iron in your baby's system can lead to anaemia, which can affect your baby's physical and mental development. The World Health Organization states that iron deficiency in young children is widespread and as such they recommend that iron-rich foods are introduced at about six months. Your baby can get iron and protein from meat and fish, and this is easily absorbed by the body. On the other hand, if you are going down the vegetarian route or you feel your baby is too young to start a meat and fish diet, you can get enough iron from dark green vegetables, broad beans, lentils, dried apricots, figs and prunes. In the case of waiting for your baby to get older before you introduce meat and fish, you can start that gradually by introducing minced meat, chicken and mashed cooked fish into the diet.

Good sources of iron for your baby include:

Liver, beef, lamb, chicken breast and thigh, sardines, lentils, chickpeas, spinach, green peas, kale, broccoli, apricots, figs, raisins and eggs.

Tip: Include a source of vitamin C as this can double the absorption of iron from cereals and legumes.

CHAPTER FIVE

HEALTH AND SAFETY

HEALTH AND SAFETY

What to Avoid

For every parent, it is exciting watching your child enjoy his solid food experience; it is even more exciting watching your little one love all the varieties and new flavours you introduce to her. However, there are certain foods that should stay off the menu for the first year. Some of the items listed below pose neither an allergy risk nor an immediate health risk, e.g., sugar and salt, but they are not well suited for babies. Here's a guide on foods to avoid during your baby's first year, along with recommendations for when it is safe to introduce them. As always, speak to your baby's GP or a nutritional therapist before introducing any of these foods.

Honey

Honey may contain spores of the bacteria *Clostridium botulinum*. Although harmless to adults, the spores can cause infant botulism in babies under one year old due to the immaturity of a baby's intestinal tract. This serious but rarely fatal illness can cause constipation, weakened sucking, poor appetite and lethargy and even potentially pneumonia and dehydration. So avoid honey until your child is at least one.

Cow's milk

As mentioned earlier, do not give your child cow's milk as a drink until he is one year old, as it cannot properly sustain an active, growing infant. It simply doesn't have all the nutritional components needed for healthy growth and development. In addition, it can be hard for young infants to digest.

Salt

Your baby does not need any added salt, and adding salt to her meals will overwhelm her young palate. Your baby's kidneys are very fragile and unable to process a high amount of added salt. Too much salt from sources other than natural foods like veggies and fruits may damage baby's kidneys and possibly even cause brain damage. Salt and salty food like cheese, bacon, sausages, chips with added salt, crisps, convenience food, takeaways, gravy and meals made with stock cubes are bad for babies, so limit these. When you do start to use stock cubes, a low sodium variety would be preferable.

Sugar

Babies who have never tried sweets don't care for them. Although your baby's taste buds do have a natural affinity for sweet foods, at this stage their palette is a blank canvas so you can pretty much build your baby's foundation the healthy way. You can save the sugary treats for your baby's first birthday or later, especially chocolate (which also contains caffeine) and sweets with a hard sugar coating, jelly beans, etc., which pose a choking hazard.

Choking Hazards

Because of the danger of choking, avoid giving your baby foods that won't dissolve in the mouth or can't be mashed with the gums. These include uncooked raisins, whole peas (unless they're mashed), raw firm-fleshed veggies (carrots, peppers) or fruit (apples, unripe pears, grapes) and chunks of meat or poultry. There are now baby safe feeders available to safely feed your baby without the risk of choking.

High-Mercury Fish

Research shows that regularly feeding fish to babies can boost IQ; this is because of the high omega-3 content. Just avoid swordfish, shark, tilefish or king mackerel, which are high in mercury. Even adults shouldn't eat these very often.

Unpasteurised Foods

Avoid unpasteurised (raw) dairy products. They can contain dangerous bacteria that can cause life-threatening illness in babies and young kids.

Baby Food Allergies

As we mentioned earlier in the book, try not to overload your baby with different types of food so that you are able to gauge whether your baby has any allergic reactions and if they do, to what foods. The foods most likely to cause allergic reactions include cow's milk, eggs, wheat, gluten, nuts, peanuts, seeds and shellfish. If you do introduce these types of food, do it a little at a time and track the symptoms with your food diary. In any case it is best not to introduce these foods before the six-month period. According to the UK National Health Service, babies are more likely to develop allergies if there is a history of eczema, asthma and hay fever in the family. It is also important to take note of any family history of food allergy or skin reactions to help you have an idea of the types of foods your baby may be allergic or intolerant to.

The most usual signs of food allergy in your baby are:

- Bloating and gassiness.
- A skin reaction like rashes, swollen lips and throat.

- Diarrhoea.

- Unusual cranky behaviour from your baby.

- Vomiting or increased spit-up.

- Breathing difficulties.

- A runny nose.

If you suspect your baby is lactose intolerant please speak to your baby's GP or a nutritional therapist.

Choking

When weaning, one of the most important things is to never leave your baby unsupervised as he could easily choke on their food.

When you're cooking, especially finger food, you want to ensure that the food is not too hard but is soft enough for your baby to mash it with his gums. Also, you want to make sure that you remove any bones from meat or fish before serving it to your baby.

What Not to Do When Your Child is Choking:

- Don't panic – stay calm. You will not achieve a lot if you are anxious.

What to Do When Your Child is Choking:

1) Back blows:

Step 1:

Place your baby face down on your thigh or arm. Support their head.

Step 2:

With the raised part of your palm nearest to your wrist (the heel), firmly slap the back at the area between the shoulder blades. Wait after each slap to check his airway is no longer blocked. You will do this about five times.

If your baby is still choking, try the chest thrust:

2) Chest thrusts:

Step 1:

Place your baby face up on your arm. Support his head.

Step 2:

With two fingers, push inwards and upwards against the lower half of your baby's breastbone.

Step 3:

Wait after each thrust to check his airway is no longer blocked.

All content here should be considered as opinion only. Always consult your healthcare provider before adopting any of the suggestions in this book, and do discuss any health conditions, food sensitivities or allergies that may require diagnosis or medical attention.

Hygiene

When you start weaning, whether you're cooking your baby's meals or using store-bought food, you need to ensure that you do the following:

- Always wash your hands before and while you are preparing your baby's food and before you feed your baby. Dry your hands using a kitchen towel, not a tea towel, which is a breeding ground for germs. It is also important to check that your baby's hands are clean.

- Clean all surfaces, especially your baby's high chair and your cooking area.

- Thoroughly clean every bit of your baby's feeding utensils.

- Wash all fruits and vegetables fed to your baby.

- Use separate chopping boards for meat and fish. The most effective way is to have different colours for meat and fish so you don't get confused.

- Don't re-use food your baby has left from another feeding, because the spoon you use transfers bacteria from your baby's mouth into the food. If you're using shop-bought food from a jar, anything your baby has not eaten should be thrown away. If using homemade food, use small storage containers so that there is just enough food for your baby to eat and you can minimise wastage.

- Check the labels of store-bought food before you feed it to your baby.

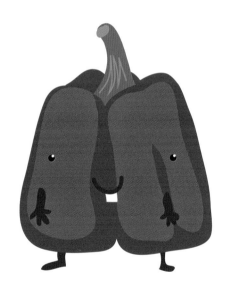

CHAPTER SIX
WEANING STAGE ONE (SIX MONTHS)

WEANING STAGE ONE

Weaning is a slow and steady process. When you know your baby is ready for solids, her first foods can include soft cooked thinly puréed fruits and vegetables or soft finger foods. To avoid your baby becoming accustomed to sweet foods, you can offer vegetable purées first. When feeding your baby, allow her to play with the food and wait for her to open her mouth. Do not force food on her. You want your baby to feel in control and comfortable. Remember to test hot foods (including the middle of the food) before offering them to your baby.

Finally, this is intended as a guide to the first few weeks of weaning, but always be guided by your baby's appetite. No two babies are alike, so some will want to go faster whereas others will take longer to move onto the next stage of weaning.

Taste

Start by introducing your baby to simple, gentle tastes. I have included some excellent first tastes of solids for your baby. After she has accepted her first tastes of single fruit or vegetable purées, you can move onto more complex fruit and vegetable combinations.

Your baby's usual milk (breast milk or formula milk) can be used to modify the texture of the food, plus it helps the transition to solids as the familiar taste might help your baby accept the unfamiliar texture.

Make sure you peel fruits and vegetables to remove any skin that may be too tough for baby.

Texture

During the first one to two weeks of introducing solids to your baby's diet, smooth purées are ideal to help her baby learn how to swallow solids and they are easy to digest. However, as the weeks progress, the texture of the food offered should progress from a runny and smooth consistency to a slighter thicker purée with no lumps toward the end of his first month.

Timing

When you begin weaning, decide which daytime feed is most relaxed for yourself and baby. I personally introduced solids to Micah after his lunchtime feed. Try to avoid introducing food to your baby when he is too hungry, as he will not be able to eat quickly enough to be satisfied, leaving him frustrated. Give him most of his milk feed first to quench his thirst and satisfy his hunger, then offer one to two teaspoonfuls of his puréed food.

Remember, at this stage your baby still needs a minimum of 600ml (20oz) of milk a day.

Quantity

When you start weaning your baby, try feeding a teaspoonful or two a day to ease her gently in. As your baby's appetite grows you can gradually increase the quantity and the number of feeds.

To avoid waste, you can make up a batch of purée and freeze in small portions using sterilised trays or pop-up freezer trays and pots.

Nutritionally Balanced Diet

No single food can give your baby all the goodness they need. So once your baby has got used to the idea of weaning, gradually start to offer him a wider variety of food. This will help ensure that he gets a good balance of nutrients, including vitamins and minerals as well as the energy he needs for all that growing and exploring. In addition, it helps to avoid your baby becoming a fussy eater.

Foods to Avoid

At this early stage of weaning, there are a few foods that your baby may develop an allergy to, and so are best avoided. Some other foods to avoid include sugary and salty food, highly processed foods, eggs, nuts, stock cubes and foods containing gluten (please check the "Foods to avoid" section). Also be aware that some fruits or vegetables may pose a choking hazard.

Do not give your baby whole cow's milk as a drink until he is one year old.

FIRST TASTES:

Apple Purée

Ingredients

- 2 apples

Directions

- Peel, core and dice the apples.

- Steam the apples for 7 minutes or until tender.

- Purée in a food processor until you get a very smooth purée (no lumps). You can add some of the steaming liquid, 1 tablespoon at a time for desired consistency.

> Nutrition: The purée is high in fibre and vitamin C and preliminary research suggests that regular apple consumption may reduce babies' risk of developing asthma.

Pear Purée

Ingredients

- 2 pears

Directions

Peel, core and dice the pears.

- Steam the pears for 7 minutes or until tender.

- Purée in a food processor or blender. You can add some of the steaming liquid, 1 tablespoon at a time for desired consistency.

> Nutrition: This purée is high in vitamin C, fibre and antioxidants and eating pears helps children to regulate their blood sugar levels.

Mashed Banana

Babies love bananas. They remain one of Micah's favourite fruits. This doesn't require cooking, it is filling and a good source of potassium.

Ingredients

- 1 ripe banana

Directions

- Peel the banana, removing all strings.

- Mash the banana with a fork.

- You can add a little of your baby's usual milk for a creamier texture.

> Nutrition: Banana is energy-dense and a good source of complex carbohydrate and potassium.

Mashed Avocado

Avocados turn black fast so it's not a convenient food to prepare in advance.

Ingredients

- 1 ripe avocado

Directions

- Cut a ripe avocado down the middle, twist the halves apart and scoop out a few spoonfuls.
- Mash with a fork and add water or your baby's usual milk a little bit at a time for desired consistency and feed immediately.

> Nutrition: Avocado is a great source of mono saturated fat, which is needed for proper brain development.

Papaya Purée

Ingredients

- ½ small ripe papaya

Directions

- Halve the papaya lengthwise. Use a spoon to scoop out the black seeds. Then peel the skin away from the flesh.
- Mash the papaya with a fork. You can mix with baby rice or your baby's usual milk to vary the texture.

> Nutrition: Papayas are a good source of beta-carotene and Vitamin C and also provide supportive enzymes to aid baby's digestion.

Mango Purée

Ingredients

- 1 ripe mango

Directions

- Peel, deseed and purée the mango until smooth.

> Nutrition: Mango purée is a good source of B vitamins including B6, which is needed for energy and vitamin A which promotes good eyesight.

Butternut Squash Purée

Ingredients

- 1 medium butternut squash

Directions

- Wash, peel, deseed and chop the butternut squash into cubes.

- Steam or boil the butternut squash for 20 minutes or until tender.

- Purée in a blender. You can add some of the steaming liquid, 1 tablespoon at a time for desired consistency.

> Nutrition: Butternut squash is very high in vitamin A and the B vitamins and provides some iron, calcium and zinc.

Sweet Potato Purée

Ingredients

- 1 medium sweet potato

Directions

- Peel and dice the sweet potato

- Steam or boil the sweet potato for 20 minutes or until tender.

- Drain and mash well, adding a little of the cooking liquid or your baby's usual milk to thin to the desired consistency.

> Nutrition: Sweet potato is a good source of vitamins A and C as well as trace minerals copper and manganese.

Carrot Purée

Ingredients

- 2 medium carrots

Directions

- Peel and dice the carrots.

- Steam the carrots for 15 minutes or until tender.

- Purée in a blender until very smooth – you can add a little of the cooking liquid or your baby's usual milk to get your desired consistency.

> Nutrition: Carrot is a very good source of vitamin K which is required for proper blood clotting.

Parsnip Purée

Parsnips purée to a lovely, creamy texture.

Ingredients

- 2 medium parsnips

Directions

- Peel and dice the parsnips.

- Steam the parsnips for 15 minutes or until tender.

- Purée in a blender. You can add a little of the cooking liquid to get your desired consistency.

Nutrition: Parsnip is an excellent source of soluble and insoluble dietary fibre that is needed for healthy digestion, as well as vitamins E and K.

Courgette Purée

Courgette purées to a very thin, almost watery consistency.

Ingredients

- 1 medium courgette

- Organic baby rice (optional)

Directions

- Remove both ends of the courgette, peel, then dice.

- You can boil in a very little water or steam them until tender.

- Purée to desired consistency. If purée is too watery you can add a teaspoon of baby rice for a thicker texture.

Nutrition: Courgette is very high in poly-phenolic antioxidants which have multiple health benefits.

AFTER YOUR BABY HAS ACCEPTED HIS FIRST TASTES:

Banana and Apple Purée

Ingredients

- 2 apples, peeled, cored and diced
- 1 ripe banana, peeled and diced

Directions

- Steam the apples until tender.
- Place the diced bananas and apples in a food processor or blender.
- Purée to desired consistency.

> Nutrition: This classic combination provides a broad range of immune boosting and energy enhancing vitamins and minerals.

Carronut Purée

Your baby will love the delicate nutty sweetness and tempting flavour of this purée.

Ingredients

- 2 medium carrots, peeled and diced
- 1 tablespoon virgin coconut oil
- ¾ cup coconut milk
- Pinch of nutmeg

Directions

- In a saucepan over a medium heat, add the coconut oil, nutmeg and diced carrots. Mix together until the carrots are well coated with coconut oil.
- Add the coconut milk and simmer on a very low heat for 20 minutes, stirring every 5 minutes or so, until carrot is tender.
- Purée to desired consistency.

> Nutrition: This combo packs a powerful nutritional punch — coconut helps provide immunity against infection and carrots, of course, are a super food for your baby too, providing plenty of beta-carotene, which your baby's body converts to vitamin A.

Creamy Mango and Banana Purée

Smooth and creamy, this was one of Micah's favourite purées. It is a no-cook recipe packed full of nutrition.

Ingredients

- 1 mango, peeled and pitted
- 1 banana, peeled and diced

- 4 tablespoons baby's usual milk
- Pinch of cinnamon

Directions

- Place the mango, banana chunks, cinnamon and milk into a food processor.
- Blend until smooth.

> Nutrition: This recipe is perfect for babies with a sweet tooth! It is energy-dense, good for digestion and contains a range of essential vitamins and minerals.

Tropical Fruit Purée

Ingredients

- 1 banana, peeled and chopped
- 1 mango, peeled, deseeded and chopped
- 1 cup chopped papaya

Directions

- Mash the banana, mango and papaya together or purée in a blender to desired consistency. There is no need to add water as papaya purées to a watery consistency.

> Nutrition: Variety is so important for your baby at this early stage and by mixing fruits together you give your baby the benefits of each. This purée can also be used effectively to relieve constipation in your baby.

Peach and Banana Purée

Ingredients

- 1 banana
- 2 peaches, skinned, stoned and chopped
- ½ teaspoon unsalted organic butter
- Pinch of cinnamon

Directions

- To skin the peach, cut a shallow "X" at the bottom. Bring water to the boil in a large saucepan. Water should be deep enough to cover the peach. Prepare an ice-water bath in a large bowl. Place the peach into the boiling water for about 45 seconds. Remove the peach and immediately place it in the ice-water bath. When the peach is blanched and cooled, it is time to peel it. Starting at the "X", remove the skin from the peach using a knife.

- Slice peaches in half, lengthwise, working your way around the pit.

- Sauté peach chunks in butter, and a pinch of cinnamon until softened.

- Mix with the banana and purée to desired consistency.

- You can add a little of the steaming liquid to get desired consistency.

> Nutrition: Peaches are rich in the fat soluble vitamins A, D, E and K which are rarely found together in fruits and vegetables. The bananas make this recipe energy-dense and packed full of potassium.

Avocado, Banana and Kiwi Purée

Ingredients

- 2 ripe kiwi fruits, peeled
- 1/2 ripe avocado
- 1 banana

Directions

- Cut off the central core from the kiwi fruit.
- Add the kiwi fruit, avocado, banana and nutmeg into blender and purée until smooth.

Nutrition: Kiwi fruits are nutrient-dense and a great way to get vitamin E and vitamin K into your baby's diet.

Plumple Purée

Ingredients

- 2 apples, peeled, cored and diced
- 2 plums, peeled, pitted and diced

Directions

- In a saucepan, simmer apples and plums together until tender.
- Purée in a blender with a little bit of the cooking water, if necessary, to get the desired consistency.

Nutrition: Plums make the iron in your baby's milk more easily absorbed and can also calm tummy-aches.

Mango Compote

Ingredients

- ½ cup dried mango
- 2 cups water
- 1 pear

Directions

- Pour warm water into a bowl, tip in the dried mango and leave to soak for an hour.
- Place the dried mango in a saucepan with water. Bring to the boil, reduce the heat and simmer for 20 minutes, stirring occasionally until the fruit has softened.
- Add the pear and simmer for another 5 minutes, until the liquid has thickened slightly.
- Purée in a blender till smooth.

Nutrition: Mango contains enzymes and a probiotic culture, both of which aid digestion. It is also a very good source of vitamins C and A.

Apple and Cinnamon Purée

Ingredients

- 2 apples, peeled and chopped into large chunks
- ⅛ teaspoon cinnamon

Directions

- Steam the apples until tender.
- Place the apples and cinnamon in a food processor and purée until smooth.

Nutrition: Cinnamon is antimicrobial and will help protect your baby against common germs. The smell of cinnamon is also thought to boost brain function – plus it tastes delicious!

Nutrition: The prunes in this recipe have a gentle laxative effect and are mildly antimicrobial so this recipe is good for relieving constipation and tummy-aches.

Pear and Prunes

A perfect combination of slightly sweet and extremely nutritious. If your baby is experiencing constipation, the prunes in this purée may help to soften stools and relieve any discomfort.

Ingredients

- 1 cup dried prunes

- 2 pears, peeled, cored and chopped

Directions

- Add water to a saucepan and pour in the prunes. Bring to a boil and simmer on a medium heat for 10 minutes. Add the pear and simmer for a further 5 minutes. Drain, reserving the cooking liquid.

- Transfer to a blender and blend until smooth, adding the desired quantity of cooking liquid as prunes tend to become a pasty, gluey consistency when puréed.

Mixed Berry and Pear Compote

Ingredients

- 1 pear, peeled, cored and diced

- 1 cup dried berry mix

- Pinch of cinnamon

Directions

- Place the berry mix and cinnamon in a saucepan with enough water to cover it. Bring to a boil and simmer for 15 minutes. Add the pear and simmer for a further 5 minutes. Reserve any leftover cooking liquid.

- Purée in a blender. You can add reserved cooking liquid to achieve the desired consistency.

Nutrition: Berries are one of the best sources of vitamin C and also provide a wide range of disease-fighting antioxidants which will keep your baby strong.

Butternut Squash and Pear

This was one of our favourite combos. Babies love the naturally sweet taste of butternut squash and it combines well with a variety of other vegetables and fruits.

Ingredients

- ½ medium butternut squash, peeled, seeded and diced

- 1 pear, peeled, cored and chopped

Directions

- Simmer or steam the butternut squash for 20 minutes.

- Add the pear and simmer for a further 5 minutes until the squash and pear are tender.

- Transfer to a food processor or blender and purée until smooth.

Nutrition: This purée contains key antioxidants that will help to support your baby's developing immune system. It is also energy-dense and a good source of vitamins C and A.

Pumpkin and Apple

This is a great alternative for mamas in countries where butternut squash is not easily available.

Ingredients

- 1 small pumpkin

- 2 apples, peeled, cored and diced

Directions

- Preheat oven to 165°C.

- Rinse the pumpkin to remove any dirt or debris.

- Cut the pumpkin in half, stem to base. Scoop out the seeds and pulp.

- Lay the pumpkin face side down in a large baking tray and fill the tray with water.

- Bake in the preheated oven for 1 hour, or until the pumpkin is tender.

- Meanwhile, steam the apples for 5 minutes or until tender.

- Remove the pumpkin from the oven and scoop out the insides, discarding the skin.

- Transfer the baked pumpkin and steamed apples to a food processor and purée until smooth.

Nutrition: Pumpkin is a good source of plant protein and omega-3 fatty acids which are vital for your baby's brain development.

Courgette and Banana

Ingredients

- 1 courgette, trimmed and chopped

- 1 banana, chopped

Directions

- Steam the courgette until tender (no need to peel it as the skin contains many nutrients and will become soft after steaming and puréeing).

- Add banana chunks and the courgette to a food processor and purée – you do not need to add any cooking liquid as the courgette purée can be watery.

Nutrition: Packed with vitamins and minerals, courgette blends well with other fruits and vegetables due to its mild taste and soft texture. The banana in this recipe helps balance the watery consistency of the courgette purée.

Apple and Carrot Purée

Ingredients

- 2 carrots, peeled and chopped
- 2 apples, peeled, cored and diced
- ¼ teaspoon fresh ginger

Directions

- Simmer the carrots and ginger for 15 minutes.

- Add the apples and simmer for a further 5 minutes, until the carrots are easily pierced with a fork. Discard the ginger.

- Purée in a food processor or blender until smooth. You can add a bit of the cooking water, 1 spoonful at a time, until you get the desired consistency.

Nutrition: The carrots in this recipe may help to keep your baby's heart healthy! This recipe is also a good source of vitamin C, beta-carotene and fibre.

Carrot and Avocado Mash

Avocado and carrots together make a lovely, creamy and sweet purée that babies love. This also makes a yummy sandwich spread for older babies and toddlers.

Ingredients

- 2 medium carrots, peeled and chopped
- ½ ripe avocado, scooped out of skin

Directions

- Steam the carrots for about 20 minutes, until carrots are easily pierced with a fork.

- Place the carrots and avocado in a food processor or blender and purée until smooth. Add a little of the cooking water, breast milk or formula while blending, if necessary, to achieve the desired consistency.

Nutrition: This recipe is an excellent source of the essential fatty acids that your baby needs for healthy brain development and vitamins C and A.

Sweet Potato and Apple

Ingredients

- 1 sweet potato, peeled and cut into chunks
- 1 apple, peeled, cored and diced

Directions

- Steam the sweet potato until tender.

- Add the apples and steam for a further 5 minutes or until tender.

- Purée in food processor. You can add a little of the steaming liquid to thin if required.

Nutrition: This recipe is energy-dense and will appeal to babies with a sweet tooth. The apple in this purée may gently relieve constipation and calm tummy-aches.

Green Apple Purée

This is a great purée for babies as the sweetness of the apple counteracts the bitterness of the kale.

Ingredients

- 2 apples, peeled, cored and diced
- ½ cup chopped kale, ribs and thick stems removed

Directions

- Steam the apples and kale until the kale begins to wilt – about 5 minutes.
- Transfer to a blender and purée until smooth.

> Nutrition: Kale boasts high levels of vitamins C and K as well as iron and calcium. Eating kale regularly will help your baby to develop strong bones – plus they love the colour!

Green Beans and Pear Purée

Ingredients

- ½ cup green beans, chopped
- 2 pears, peeled, cored and chopped

Directions

- Steam the green beans until tender.
- Add the pear and steam for a further 5 minutes.
- Transfer to a blender and purée until smooth.
- If needed, you can put through a fine sieve to get rid of the hulls.

> Nutrition: Green beans are rich in vitamin A and fibre and are a wonderfully nutritious addition to a baby's diet.

Sweet Pea Purée

Ingredients

- 2 ripe pears, peeled, cored and chopped
- 1 cup of frozen peas

Directions

- In a saucepan of boiling water, place the peas and cook until very tender. Add the pears and simmer for a further 5 minutes.

- Place the pears and peas in a blender and purée until smooth. Use a setting to make it as fine as possible as green pea skins are rather difficult to completely purée.

Nutrition: Peas provide a unique assortment of phytonutrients and make this recipe anti-inflammatory and rich in antioxidants.

Nutrition: Beetroots are an excellent source of folic acid and a very good source of fibre, manganese and potassium and the purple colour of beetroot makes it a fun and visually appealing food for your little one. Don't be surprised if your baby's urine has a slight red tinge after eating this purée. It's perfectly normal and healthy.

Beet Purée

Beetroot stains – so make sure you cover your little one's clothes and surroundings when feeding beets.

Ingredients

- 2 small beetroot
- 1 pear, peeled and diced
- ¼ teaspoon chopped basil

Directions

- Rinse the beets in cold water, remove stalks, peel and cut into cubes.
- In a small saucepan, cook the beets in a scant amount of water until tender.
- Meanwhile, steam the pear until tender.
- Blend all the ingredients together to desired consistency.

Carrot and Mango Purée

Ingredients

- 2 carrots, peeled and chopped
- 1 mango, peeled, deseeded and chopped

Directions

- Steam the carrots until tender.
- Purée the mango and carrots until you get the desired texture.

> Nutrition: This purée has a heavenly flavour, is an antioxidant powerhouse and provides impressive amounts of vitamins C and A.

Parsnip and Carrot Purée

Ingredients

- 1 teaspoon unsalted organic butter
- 1 tablespoon minced shallot
- 2 carrots, peeled and chopped
- 2 parsnips, peeled and chopped
- ½ teaspoon chopped fresh thyme
- low salt vegetable stock

Directions

- Melt butter in a saucepan; add the shallot and sauté for 5 minutes until softened. Add the carrots, parsnip and thyme and sauté for about 5 minutes. Add enough vegetable stock to cover.
- Bring to a boil and simmer until vegetables are tender – about 15 to 20 minutes.
- Purée in a food processor, adding cooking liquid, 1 tablespoon at a time if needed, to reach the desired consistency.

> Nutrition: This purée is energy-dense for hungry babies and provides good levels of vitamin C to boost your baby's immune system and beta-carotene for their eye development.

Sweet Potato, Broccoli and Carrot

Ingredients

- 1 sweet potato, peeled and finely chopped
- 1 carrot, peeled and finely chopped
- 1 cup broccoli florets

Directions

- Boil or steam the sweet potato and carrots for 15 minutes.
- Add the broccoli and boil or steam for a further 5 minutes until the vegetables are tender.
- Purée in food processor until smooth.

Nutrition: Broccoli supports your baby's developing liver and the supporting nutrients in broccoli help baby to absorb and store vitamin D.

Cauliflower and Sweet Potato Coconut Purée

Ingredients

- 1 medium sweet potato, peeled and chopped
- 1 cup of cauliflower
- ¼ cup of coconut milk
- 1 teaspoon of organic unsalted butter

Directions

- Add the potatoes to a saucepan of water. Cook for 15 minutes.
- Add cauliflower and cook for a further 5 minutes.
- Add the cooked mixture, coconut milk and butter to a food processor. Purée to desired consistency.

Nutrition: This combination is a good source of protein, folate and vitamin A.

Mixed Vegetable Medley

Ingredients

- ½ cup red pepper, deseeded and chopped
- ½ cup sweetcorn
- ½ cup frozen peas
- ½ cup small courgette, chopped
- 1 teaspoon organic unsalted butter

Directions

- Steam the pepper for 10 minutes.
- Add the sweetcorn, peas, and courgette and steam for a further 10 minutes or until the vegetables are tender.
- Purée in a blender, adding the butter.

Nutrition: The addition of butter to this purée makes the vitamins in the vegetables more easily absorbed. It is also rich in vitamins C, A, E, K and folate.

Baked Sweet Potatoes

This was one of Micah's favourite purées and he still enjoys it to this day. It is delicious, healthy and so easy to prepare.

Ingredients

- 1 sweet potato
- 1 teaspoon vegetable oil
- 1 tablespoon organic unsalted butter

Directions

- Preheat the oven to 190°C.
- Scrub the potatoes and prick with a fork.
- Rub vegetable oil all over the potato.
- Bake for 45 to 60 minutes until tender.
- Cool potato just until it can be handled, split the potato and scoop out the flesh with a spoon.
- Blend or mash the sweet potato, adding butter until smooth.

Nutrition: Baked sweet potatoes are a good source of vitamins A and C as well as trace minerals copper and manganese. The addition of butter makes the beta-carotene in the sweet potato far more absorbable.

Carrot and Sweet Potato with Peas

Ingredients

- 1 carrot, peeled and chopped
- 1 sweet potato, peeled and chopped
- ½ cup frozen peas

Directions

- Place the carrots and sweet potatoes in a saucepan.
- Add enough water to just cover the vegetables and simmer for 10 minutes.
- Add the peas and simmer for a further 10 minutes.
- Purée in a blender. It is best to use the setting that makes the finest liquid purées as pea skins are rather difficult to completely purée.
- Add the cooking water as necessary to achieve the desired consistency.

Nutrition: The vitamin C in the carrots makes the folate and iron in the peas more accessible to baby and pea skins are an excellent source of roughage.

Broccoli and Cauliflower Purée

Ingredients

- 1 cup broccoli florets
- 1 cup cauliflower florets

Directions

- Steam the broccoli and cauliflower until they are tender.
- Purée in a blender to desired consistency.

Nutrition: This combination of brassica vegetables is a good source of iron and vitamin C and will support your baby's liver function.

Carrot, Broccoli and Butternut Squash

Ingredients

- 1 medium carrot, peeled and diced
- 1 cup of broccoli florets
- ½ butternut squash, peeled and diced
- 2 cups low salt vegetable stock

Directions

- Add the butternut squash, carrots and stock to a saucepan. Bring to a boil and simmer for about 15 minutes.
- Add broccoli and cook for a further 5 minutes.
- Blend all three to your desired consistency. You can add a little of the cooking liquid.

> Nutrition: This is a great blood-strengthening purée, which provides a good source of vitamin C, folate and iron.

Celery, Leek and Potato Purée

Ingredients

- 1¼ cup potatoes, peeled and diced
- ½ celery stalk, diced
- 1 leek, trimmed and diced
- ½ small onion, diced
- 1 teaspoon unsalted butter
- 1 low salt organic chicken cube

Directions

- Melt the butter in a large saucepan. Sauté the onion for 5 minutes or until it has turned translucent.
- Add the potatoes, celery and leek and chicken stock cube. Pour in just enough water to cover the vegetables. Bring to the boil, reduce heat and let it simmer for 20 minutes or until the vegetables are tender.
- Purée in a blender, using the stock to get the desired consistency.

> Nutrition: Packed with antioxidants from the celery, this purée is antimicrobial and a good source of vitamin C and fibre.

My First Okra Soup

Babies love okra soup because of the gooey texture when cooked. It is also delicious and packed full of vitamins. This basic okra soup serves as an introduction to the varieties of okra soup in the book. I introduced okra earlier to my son at six months, because he was such an enthusiastic eater, and he loved it.

Ingredients

- 175g okra
- ½ tablespoon ground crayfish
- ⅛ cup finely diced onions
- 1 tablespoon palm oil
- 1 low salt organic beef stock cube

Directions

- Wash and chop the okra. Add the chopped okra and 2 cups water to a blender.
- In a saucepan, add the blended okra, onions, palm oil, crayfish and beef stock cube.
- Cook on medium heat, uncovered for about 10 minutes or until okra is cooked.

Nutrition: A good source of vitamins A, C, B (complex), and E, all of which play an important role in your baby's physical and mental development. Okra has a gentle laxative effect and therefore reduces the risk of constipation.

Stage One: Six Months, Week One

	Early Morning (5am)	Breakfast (7/7.30am)	Lunch (11.15/11.30am)	
Monday	Breastfeed or formula milk	Breastfeed or formula milk	Breastfeed or formula milk, 1–2 teaspoons of mashed banana	
Tuesday	Breastfeed or formula milk	Breastfeed or formula milk	Breastfeed or formula milk, 1–2 teaspoons of mashed banana	
Wednesday	Breastfeed or formula milk	Breastfeed or formula milk	Breastfeed or formula milk, 1–2 teaspoons of carrot purée	
Thursday	Breastfeed or formula milk	Breastfeed or formula milk	Breastfeed or formula, 1–2 teaspoons of carrot purée	
Friday	Breastfeed or formula milk	Breastfeed or formula milk	Breastfeed or formula, 1–2 teaspoons of avocado purée	
Saturday	Breastfeed or formula milk	Breastfeed or formula milk	Breastfeed or formula, 1–2 teaspoons of avocado purée	
Sunday	Breastfeed or formula milk	Breastfeed or formula milk	Breastfeed or formula, 1–2 teaspoons of apple purée	

Mealtime should include water in a beaker for baby.

If you must, offer a small amount of juice from a cup rather than a bottle, offering it only with meals. Dilute the juice (the UK's NHS recommends one part juice to ten parts water), or try using juice just to flavour the water.

WEEKLY MENU PLANS

Mid-afternoon (2.30pm)	Tea (5pm)	Bedtime (6.30pm)
Breastfeed or formula milk	Breastfeed or formula milk	Breastfeed or formula milk
Breastfeed or formula milk	Breastfeed or formula milk	Breastfeed or formula milk
Breastfeed or formula milk	Breastfeed or formula milk	Breastfeed or formula milk
Breastfeed or formula milk	Breastfeed or formula milk	Breastfeed or formula milk
Breastfeed or formula milk	Breastfeed or formula milk	Breastfeed or formula milk
Breastfeed or formula milk	Breastfeed or formula milk	Breastfeed or formula milk
Breastfeed or formula milk	Breastfeed or formula milk	Breastfeed or formula milk

Stage One: Six Months, Week Two

	Early Morning (5am)	Breakfast (7/7.30am)	Lunch (11.15/11.30am)	
Monday	Breastfeed or formula milk	Breastfeed or formula milk	Breastfeed or formula milk, Parsnip and Carrot	
Tuesday	Breastfeed or formula milk	Breastfeed or formula milk	Breastfeed or formula milk, Parsnip and Carrot	
Wednesday	Breastfeed or formula milk	Breastfeed or formula milk	Breastfeed or formula milk, Butternut Squash and Pear Purée	
Thursday	Breastfeed or formula milk	Breastfeed or formula milk	Breastfeed or formula milk, Butternut Squash and Pear Purée	
Friday	Breastfeed or formula milk	Breastfeed or formula milk	Breastfeed or formula milk, Courgette and Banana Purée	
Saturday	Breastfeed or formula milk	Breastfeed or formula milk	Breastfeed or formula milk, Beet Purée	
Sunday	Breastfeed or formula milk	Breastfeed or formula milk	Breastfeed or formula milk, Courgette and Banana Purée	

Mid-afternoon (2.30pm)	Tea (5pm)	Bedtime (6.30pm)
Breastfeed or formula milk	Breastfeed or formula milk	Breastfeed or formula milk
Breastfeed or formula milk	Breastfeed or formula milk	Breastfeed or formula milk
Breastfeed or formula milk	Breastfeed or formula milk	Breastfeed or formula milk
Breastfeed or formula milk	Breastfeed or formula milk	Breastfeed or formula milk
Breastfeed or formula milk	Breastfeed or formula milk	Breastfeed or formula milk
Breastfeed or formula milk	Breastfeed or formula milk	Breastfeed or formula milk
Breastfeed or formula milk	Breastfeed or formula milk	Breastfeed or formula milk

Stage One: Six Months, Week Three

	Early Morning (5am)	Breakfast (7/7.30am)	Lunch (11.15/11.30am)	
Monday	Breastfeed or formula milk	Breastfeed or formula milk, Apple and Cinnamon	Breastfeed or formula milk, Broccoli and Cauliflower	
Tuesday	Breastfeed or formula milk	Breastfeed or formula milk, baby rice	Breastfeed or formula milk, Mixed Vegetable Medley	
Wednesday	Breastfeed or formula milk	Breastfeed or formula milk, Tropical Fruit Purée	Breastfeed or formula milk, Watercress, Potato and Parsnip	
Thursday	Breastfeed or formula milk	Breastfeed or formula milk, Banana and Apple Purée	Breastfeed or formula milk, baked sweet potato	
Friday	Breastfeed or formula milk	Breastfeed or formula milk, mashed avocado	Breastfeed or formula milk, Carronut Purée	
Saturday	Breastfeed or formula milk	Breastfeed or formula milk, Papaya with Baby Rice	Breastfeed or formula milk, Watercress, Potato and Parsnip	
Sunday	Breastfeed or formula milk	Breastfeed or formula milk, Mango Compote	Breastfeed or formula milk, Mixed Vegetable Medley	

Mid-afternoon (2.30pm)	Tea (5pm)	Bedtime (6.30pm)
Breastfeed or formula milk	Breastfeed or formula milk	Breastfeed or formula milk
Breastfeed or formula milk	Breastfeed or formula milk	Breastfeed or formula milk
Breastfeed or formula milk	Breastfeed or formula milk	Breastfeed or formula milk
Breastfeed or formula milk	Breastfeed or formula milk	Breastfeed or formula milk
Breastfeed or formula milk	Breastfeed or formula milk	Breastfeed or formula milk
Breastfeed or formula milk	Breastfeed or formula milk	Breastfeed or formula milk
Breastfeed or formula milk	Breastfeed or formula milk	Breastfeed or formula milk

Stage One: Six Months, Week Four

	Early Morning (5am)	Breakfast (7/7.30am)	Lunch (11.15/11.30am)	
Monday	Breastfeed or formula milk, Peaches and Banana	Breastfeed or formula milk	Carrot, Broccoli and Butternut Squash, water from a beaker	
Tuesday	Breastfeed or formula milk, Mixed Berry Compote	Breastfeed or formula milk	Sweet Potato, Broccoli and Carrot Purée, water from a beaker	
Wednesday	Breastfeed or formula milk, Pear Purée	Breastfeed or formula milk	Celery, Leek and Potatoes, water from a beaker	
Thursday	Breastfeed or formula milk, mashed banana	Breastfeed or formula milk	Carrot, Broccoli and Butternut Squash, water from a beaker	
Friday	Breastfeed or formula milk, Mixed Berry Compote	Breastfeed or formula milk	Peas, Courgette and Sweet Potato, water from a beaker	
Saturday	Breastfeed or formula milk, Papaya Purée	Breastfeed or formula milk	Broccoli and Cauliflower, water from a beaker	
Sunday	Breastfeed or formula milk, Mixed Berry Compote	Breastfeed or formula milk	Parsnips and carrots, water from a beaker	

Mid-afternoon (2.30pm)	Tea (5pm)	Bedtime (6.30pm)
Breastfeed or formula milk	Green Apple Purée, water from a beaker	Breastfeed or formula milk
Breastfeed or formula milk	Sweet Pea Purée, water from a beaker	Breastfeed or formula milk
Breastfeed or formula milk	Apple and Carrot Purée, water from a beaker	Breastfeed or formula milk
Breastfeed or formula milk	Sweet Pea Purée, water from a beaker	Breastfeed or formula milk
Breastfeed or formula milk	Carrot and Avocado Mash, water from a beaker	Breastfeed or formula milk
Breastfeed or formula milk	Green Apple Purée, water from a beaker	Breastfeed or formula milk
Breastfeed or formula milk	Courgette and Banana Mash, water from a beaker	Breastfeed or formula milk

CHAPTER SEVEN

WEANING STAGE TWO (SEVEN TO NINE MONTHS)

WEANING STAGE TWO

We started on proteins around seven months when my son had tried a variety of different vegetables. Once your baby is well adapted to his first tastes of solids, you can broaden his repertoire of daily dishes by introducing new flavours.

Since babies are receptive to new tastes it is important to offer your baby a wide variety of healthy foods from the different food groups (carbohydrates, protein, dairy, fruit and vegetables) to help him learn to love different flavours. This is because, by the age of two, these preferences may become relatively fixed until babies are around eight years old, so introducing more foods now will help to prevent them from becoming fussy eaters.

At this stage of weaning you should be aiming to establish three good solid meals a day so that by the time your baby reaches nine months of age, she is getting most of her nourishment from solids.

By the end of nine months, try to encourage your baby to drink all of his breakfast milk from a beaker. Apart from his bedtime milk, all other milk feeds and drinks should ideally be from a beaker.

Nutrition

Once your baby is well established on a variety of fruit and vegetable purées, you can slowly start to introduce proteins. The introduction of iron-rich foods like beef, chicken, and turkey is important at this stage.

During the second stage of weaning, the amount of milk your baby drinks will gradually reduce as her intake of solids increases. However, milk is still an important part of your baby's diet and she will need around 500 to 600ml a day, including the milk you use to make her food.

Food Texture

After a few weeks of getting the hang of solids, you can try moving your baby onto the second stage of weaning. This second stage of weaning involves learning how to chew. You can achieve this by progressing from smooth purées to lumpier/mashed food textures that encourage your baby to start chewing. Once she has the hang of this, she will be ready for bigger lumps and pieces.

Your baby's coordination may also be improving, so try introducing her to soft finger foods and the fun of feeding herself. You can start with:

- Soft fruit pieces, e.g., mango, melon, banana, ripe pear, peach, papaya and avocado.

- Cooked vegetable sticks, e.g., carrot, courgette and sweet potato.

- Cooked vegetable pieces, e.g., cauliflower and broccoli florets.

- Crusts of bread or toast.

- Cheese cubes.

- Roasted soft vegetable sticks, e.g. potato, sweet potato, parsnip, pepper, carrot, courgette.

At this stage, fruit need not be cooked; it can be grated or mashed. Do not worry if your baby has no teeth, as babies will chew with their gums if required.

What to Feed Your Baby

Continue to avoid foods with sugars and salt. While baby may not be too keen on many of these new foods, variety is important. Avoiding savoury foods now will only make introducing them later even harder.

Fruits

You can now introduce citrus fruit and berries, but do monitor your baby as these may cause a reaction in some children. To avoid choking, remove the pith from citrus fruit and sieve seeds from berries.

Vegetables

Start to expand your baby's repertoire of vegetables, offering as many types and colours as possible. Try to introduce veggies like aubergine and mushrooms.

Seeds, Ground Nuts and Nut Products

As long as there is no close family history of allergies, hay fever, asthma or eczema, you can try your baby with ground nut and seed products at this stage. For example, smooth peanut butter or hummus, which contains tahini (sesame seed purée). I had an experience with Micah when he turned two: he was OK the first time he had cashew nuts but had a severe allergic reaction the second time he tried them. So watch closely for reactions every time you give these foods to your baby, as some allergies don't develop at the first exposure.

Beans and Pulses

Lentils, split peas, butter beans and other pulses are a good source of iron and protein. They can be hard for young babies to digest but you can introduce them in small amounts at this stage, making sure they are well puréed or mashed.

Bread and Cereals

You can now introduce bread, rusks, pasta and breakfast cereals to your baby, with little risk of triggering an allergy.

Dairy Produce

Full-fat dairy foods such as yoghurt, fromage frais, cottage cheese, cream cheese and mild, hard cheeses like Edam and Cheddar are a good source of calories, calcium, vitamin D and protein. Small amounts of unsalted butter can be used in cooking. Full-fat cow's milk can be used in cooking, but should not be given as a drink until one year.

Eggs

As long as they are well cooked until solid, eggs can now be offered hard-boiled or used in recipes, such as omelette or scrambled eggs.

Fish

Fish is a great first protein for your baby as it contains all nine amino acids. This means that fish is one of the few sources of complete protein. Our bodies do not make amino acids; we must get them from the foods we eat. Offering your little one fish is a very healthy and nutritious option to get in some omega-3s. Fish is an amazing source of pure omega-3s, not to mention all sorts of other wonderfully healthy nutrients that growing babies need. Try blending it with green vegetables or a cheese sauce. Start with a mild white fish, like cod, and be extremely careful to remove any skin or bones. I have found bones in many pieces of fish sold as "boneless" – so check before cooking and again afterwards. Sometimes the bones are easier to spot when the fish is cooked.

Canned fish such as tuna can also be included, but make sure you choose fish in vegetable oil rather than brine, as fish in brine has a higher salt content.

Meat and Poultry

These can be offered now but must be well cooked. The texture of meat can be challenging for young babies, especially those without teeth, so you should choose tender cuts. Cook it until it is soft, and, during the early stages of introducing meat to your baby, it is best to completely purée it. In addition to making it more digestible for your little one, it minimises the choking hazard for younger babies. You can gradually firm up the texture as he gets older and more adept at chewing. And while it is great to introduce your baby to a variety of meat dishes, avoid giving salty meats such as bacon, ham and sausages to under-ones, as their kidneys are not yet able to process salt.

Chicken is high in protein and iron. It is one of the most easily digested of the meats you will feed to your baby. Chicken is most often recommended to be baby's first meat. Turkey, like chicken, is high in protein and iron and also makes a great first meat for baby.

Drinks

Offer a small amount of water from a cup at mealtimes – filtered water rather than bottled water. Your baby won't need a lot – just a few sips – but it's good to get him used to the taste and learning to drink from a cup.

You can offer diluted fruit juices (one part juice to ten parts water at mealtimes) but definitely avoid fizzy pop and sugary drinks.

Strategy

My strategy for introducing my son to proteins was to start with a larger proportion of vegetables to fish/meat for a subtler flavour. Once he was happily accepting his meat and fish, I gradually reduced the proportion of vegetables, while increasing the proportion of meat and fish.

Another strategy I adopted for introducing protein to my son was to give him protein at lunchtime and a vegetable purée at tea/dinner. I did this because it gave him enough time before bed to digest the protein meal. At around ten months, I started to alternate protein between lunch and dinner.

Basic Scrambled Eggs

This easy egg favourite is a great way to introduce your little one to eggs. It also makes a great finger food for younger babies.`

Ingredients

- 1 medium egg
- 30ml milk
- ¼ teaspoon chopped fresh chives
- 1 teaspoon unsalted butter

> Nutrition: Eggs are a top source of complete protein and in addition egg yolks provide cholesterol required for mental development and vitamin D.

Directions

- Lightly whisk the egg, milk and chives in bowl until blended.

- Heat the butter in a non-stick frying pan over a medium heat until melted. Don't allow the butter to brown or it will discolour the eggs.

- Pour in the egg mixture and let it sit, without stirring, for 30 seconds. As the mixture begins to set, stir with a wooden spoon, pulling, lifting and folding. Repeat until egg is thickened/well done and no visible liquid egg remains.

Plain Omelette

This simple omelette is delicious and great for breakfast. As your child grows older there is no limit to the number of fillings you can use with this basic omelette recipe.

Ingredients

- 2 large eggs
- ½ teaspoon unsalted butter

Directions

- Crack the eggs into a small bowl and whisk gently.

- Heat the butter in a small non-stick frying pan and pour in the eggs.

- Move the pan around to spread the egg evenly.

- In the first 30 seconds of cooking, use a spatula to create small cuts through the omelette (this allows the uncooked egg on the top to flow down to the bottom of the pan).

- If using fillings (such as cheese, finely grated orange pepper, courgette or carrots), when the top is nearly set, sprinkle any fillings over half of the omelette.

- Ease around the edge of the omelette with a spatula, then fold it in half.

- When it starts to turn golden brown underneath, remove the pan from the heat. Cut up in small pieces and leave to cool.

Nutrition: This recipe is a great source of protein, cholesterol and vitamin D. Organic free range eggs also provide some omega-3 fatty acids which are vital for proper brain development.

Caramelized Peach, Apple, Banana and Shallots

Ingredients

- ½ teaspoon unsalted organic butter
- 1 teaspoon chopped shallots
- 1 peach, skinned, stoned and chopped
- 1 apple, peeled, cored and diced
- 1 ripe banana, peeled and diced

Directions

- Heat butter in saucepan over medium heat. Add the shallots and toss to coat. Cook over medium heat for 5 minutes, tossing occasionally, until the shallots start to brown.
- Add the peach and apples and cook, stirring occasionally, until caramelized. Add banana and cook for a further 3 minutes.
- Allow to cool slightly then purée until you have your desired consistency.

Nutrition: This recipe is rich in the potassium your baby needs to break down and use carbohydrates and which helps to build muscle. The fruits in this recipe also provide trace minerals, vitamin C and fibre.

Pear Cinnamon Cereal

Ingredients

- 2 large pears, peeled, cored and diced
- Pinch of cinnamon, to taste
- Baby rice, as needed

Directions

- Steam the pear until soft.
- Add a pinch of cinnamon to taste.
- Purée until smooth. Mix with your usual baby rice.

Nutrition: This recipe can help to relieve constipation and tummy-aches in babies and the pinch of cinnamon adds spice to this otherwise simple purée.

Nutrition: The addition of yoghurt to this purée provides protein, calcium and iron, all of which are vital for your baby during this rapid stage of growth.

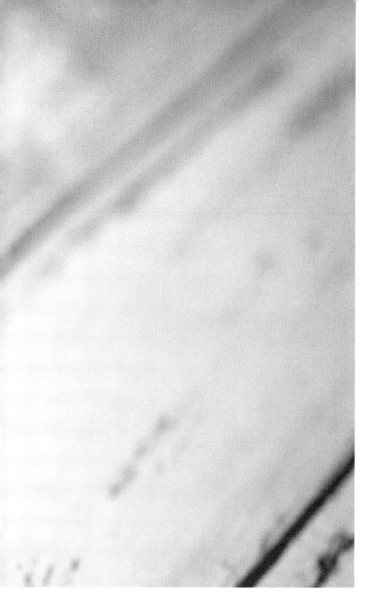

Apple and Cinnamon Yoghurt

Ingredients

- 1 teaspoon unsalted butter
- 1 apple, peeled, cored and diced
- Pinch of cinnamon, to taste
- ½ cup water
- 1 cup Greek yoghurt
- 1 teaspoon maple syrup

Directions

- Heat the butter in a saucepan. Add the apple, coating it in the butter and cook for 2 minutes.
- Add cinnamon and water and simmer for a further 3 minutes or until the apple is soft.
- Let the mixture cool slightly then purée in a blender until you have your desired consistency.
- Mix in the Greek yoghurt after the apples have cooled.

Vanilla Custard

Homemade custard can be delicious and nutritious as you can avoid artificial ingredients and control the amount of sugar you add. For babies and young toddlers, you can omit the sugar altogether.

Ingredients

- 2 cups milk
- 45ml double cream
- 1 teaspoon vanilla extract
- 2 tablespoon sugar (optional)
- 3 egg yolks
- 1 tablespoon cornflour

Directions

- In a saucepan, bring the milk, cream, vanilla extract and sugar (if using for older children) to simmering point slowly over a low heat.

- Place the egg yolks and cornflour in a large separate bowl and whisk well to combine.

- Slowly pour in half of the milk mixture into the egg yolks, whisking continuously.

- Return the milk and egg mixture to the saucepan with the remaining milk and cook over a low to medium heat, whisking continuously, making sure the custard doesn't stick to the bottom. Once the custard starts thickening, take it off the heat.

- Serve immediately or store in the fridge for up to 2 days.

Nutrition: This custard is high in protein, essential fatty acids and cholesterol, which are all vital for your baby's development at this stage.

Avocado and Cucumber Breakfast

Ingredients

- 1 medium cucumber, peeled, seeded and diced

- 1 large avocado, peeled and diced

Directions

- Purée the cucumber and avocado in a blender.

Nutrition: This purée is packed with healthy fats from the avocado, which make the vitamins A, D, E and K from the cucumber easy for your baby to absorb — an excellent start to the day.

Bananacado

This is a winning, nutritious combination for growing babies.

Ingredients

- ½ avocado, chopped
- 1 banana, chopped

Directions

- Combine the avocado and banana in a bowl and mash together with a fork until you get your desired consistency.

- If you find the mixture a little too thick, you can add a tablespoon of water or your baby's usual milk to thin the purée.

Nutrition: This combination is packed with B vitamins for energy and essential fats and trace minerals for brain development and neurological function.

Apples, Pears and Blueberries

Ingredients

- ½ cup fresh blueberries
- 1 sweet apple, peeled, cored and diced
- 1 ripe pear, peeled, cored and diced
- Organic baby rice for thickening (optional)

Directions

- Wash and remove any stems from the blueberries.

- Steam the apple, pear and blueberries for about 5 minutes or until tender.

- Transfer steamed fruits to blender and purée until smooth. This combination of fruits can purée to a watery consistency. You can add 1 to 2 tablespoons of baby rice to give this purée a thicker consistency.

Nutrition: The blueberries in this purée are an antioxidant powerhouse as well as providing vitamins K, C and manganese.

Apple Strawberry Purée

Your baby will love the taste of this and benefit from nutrients like potassium and fibre. The apples tone down the sharp flavour of the strawberries.

Ingredients

- 2 apples, peeled, cored and diced
- 1 cup strawberries, hulled and chopped
- 1 teaspoon vanilla essence
- 1 cup water

Directions

- Place the apples, strawberries and vanilla essence in a saucepan with the water and simmer for 5 minutes.
- Place in a food processor and blend.

Nutrition: This recipe is a good source of vitamin C, folate and potassium as well as providing both soluble and insoluble fibre, which promote optimum gut health.

Pear and Raspberry

This purée is simple to make and naturally sweet.

Ingredients

- 2 pears, peeled, cored and diced
- 1 cup raspberries
- 1 cup water

Directions

- Place the pear and raspberries in a small saucepan with water. Simmer for 5 minutes.
- Add the fruit to a blender and purée to desired consistency.

Nutrition: This purée is packed with antioxidants and special compounds called anthocyanins, which support your baby's liver function.

Summer Berry Purée

This purée can be a little watery due to the nature of the fruits. You can thicken the purée with a little bit of baby rice.

Ingredients

- 1 cup fresh blueberries
- 1 cup fresh strawberries
- 1 cup fresh raspberries
- 1 teaspoon vanilla essence
- ½ cup water
- Baby rice, optional

Directions

- Wash and remove any stalks from the blueberries, strawberries and raspberries.
- Simmer the fruits with water for 3 minutes.
- Blend until you reach the required consistency.
- If using, stir in the baby rice to the mixture.

Nutrition: All berries are good sources of vitamins and antioxidants. By combining these three berries you ensure that your baby receives all the amazing health benefits in one go!

Peachy Yoghurt

Greek yoghurt has become more popular in recent years for its added nutritional benefits and proportions of protein. It has a thicker consistency than regular yoghurt.

Ingredients

- 1 peach, skinned, stoned and chopped
- 1 cup Greek yoghurt
- 1 tablespoon maple syrup

Directions

- In a saucepan, add the peach and stir over a medium heat for 5 minutes until the peaches begin to break down.
- Purée the peaches in a food processor or blender until smooth.
- Mix in the Greek yoghurt and maple syrup after the peaches have cooled.

Nutrition: The peaches in this recipe provide the fat soluble vitamins A, D, E and K which are rarely found together in fruit, while the yoghurt provides protein and calcium.

Blueberry, Banana and Greek Yoghurt

Ingredients

- ½ cup blueberries
- 1 small banana
- 4 tablespoons Greek yoghurt

Directions

- Add enough water to cover the blueberries and simmer for 5 minutes until soft.
- Add the banana, blueberries and yoghurt to a blender and whizz until smooth.

Nutrition: This recipe is a good source of vitamin C, potassium, antioxidants, protein and calcium.

Rice Porridge

Rice porridge is a great way to introduce new texture to your baby's food.

Ingredients

- 1 cup basmati rce
- 1 spring onion, finely diced (optional)
- ¼ green bell pepper, finely diced
- 2 button mushrooms, finely diced
- 6 cups vegetable stock
- 1 teaspoon soy sauce (omit for younger babies)
- 1 teaspoon coconut oil
- 1 egg

Directions

- Heat the coconut oil in a saucepan, sauté the spring onion, mushroom and carrots for 5 minutes or until onion is translucent. Add the vegetable stock, rice and bell pepper. Bring to a boil, then simmer on low heat, stirring occasionally for 45 minutes.

- Add the soy sauce, break your egg and mix into the rice. Continue cooking for another 15 minutes, until rice breaks down and the mixture is thick and "creamy" when you stir it.

Nutrition: Rice is a good source of complex carbohydrate, which your baby requires for energy and growth. However, rice should be limited to two portions each week because it can contain high levels of inorganic arsenic compared to other grains.

Ripe Plantain Mash

Ingredients

- 1 ripe plantain
- Low salt vegetable stock
- 1 tablespoon of butter
- 1 teaspoon finely diced onion
- ¼ teaspoon minced garlic
- Pinch of ground cumin

Directions

- Peel the plantain and cut in half, lengthwise.
- Remove the centre where the seeds are located and chop.
- Add enough vegetable stock to cover the plantain and boil until very tender.
- Meanwhile, melt butter over medium heat, add the onions, garlic and ground cumin, cook for about 5 minutes or until onions soften.

- Add the plantain to the butter mixture and mash with a fork.

- You can add a little of the cooking liquid to get your desired consistency.

> Nutrition: This is an extremely energy-dense purée that is also rich in vitamin C, B (complex) and potassium, all of which support hormone production.

Creamy Cauliflower and Potato

Ingredients

- 1 teaspoon unsalted butter

- ½ small onion, peeled and finely chopped

- 1 cup peeled and diced potatoes

- 1 cup cauliflower florets

- 1 cup low salt chicken stock

- ½ cup double cream

Directions

- Heat butter in a saucepan. Add onions and cook until translucent, usually about 5 minutes.

- Add the potato and stock. Bring to a boil then reduce heat and simmer for about 10 minutes. Add cauliflower and simmer for another 10 minutes or until vegetables are tender. Stir in cream and take off the heat.

- Purée in a blender until you have your desired consistency.

> Nutrition: This recipe is a good source of saturated fat, which babies need for proper growth and brain development. It is also rich in vitamins C, K and folate.

Lentils and Vegetables

Lentils are a great way to add protein to your baby's diet. This is a useful recipe as you can use it as a base to add other ingredients such as beef, chicken or rice.

Ingredients

- 1 tablespoon vegetable oil
- 1 small onion, peeled and finely chopped
- ¼ teaspoon mild curry powder
- 1 carrot, peeled and finely chopped
- ½ celery stalk, diced
- 1 cup red split lentils
- 1 small parsnip, peeled and finely chopped
- 4 cups low salt vegetable stock

Directions

- Heat oil in a saucepan, add the onions, carrots and celery and cook for 5 minutes or until softened.
- Add the lentils, parsnips and vegetable stock. Bring to a boil, reduce heat and simmer covered for about 30 minutes or until the vegetables are soft.
- Purée in a blender.

Nutrition: This energy-dense recipe provides a good source of iron, protein, fibre and vitamin C.

Beet, Potato and Spinach Purée

Ingredients

- 1 teaspoon butter
- ½ small yellow onion, diced
- 1 cup peeled, diced potato
- 1 beetroot, peeled and chopped
- 2 cups low salt beef stock
- ½ cup chopped spinach

Directions

- Melt the butter in a saucepan and sauté the onion for 5 minutes or until translucent.

- Add potatoes, beets and stock. Bring to a boil and simmer for 15 minutes.

- Add the spinach and simmer for a further 5 minutes or until potatoes are tender.

- Purée the beets and potatoes, adding a little cooking liquid to achieve the desired consistency.

Nutrition: Beets contain a wonderful amount of calcium, potassium and even vitamin A.

Leek, Sweet Potato and Cauliflower

Ingredients

- 1 medium leek, white and light green parts only
- 1 tablespoon coconut oil
- 1 sweet potato, peeled and diced
- 2 cups low salt vegetable stock
- 1 cup cauliflower florets

Directions

- Cut the leeks in half lengthwise, and then chop. Swirl them around in a bowl of cold water to clean them.

- Heat the coconut oil in a saucepan and sauté the leek until soft.

- Add the sweet potato and stock. Bring to a boil, reduce the heat and simmer for 15 minutes. Add the cauliflower and simmer for a further 5 minutes until the potato is soft.

- Purée in a blender.

Nutrition: Leeks are a wonderful source of nutrition — high in vitamin C, folate, iron and potassium. The green part has beta-carotene to help with the development of your baby's eyes.

Butternut Squash and Lentils Goodness

This purée is delicious, hearty and colourful. My son loved it.

Ingredients

- 1 tablespoon coconut oil
- ½ onion, peeled and diced
- ½ medium butternut squash, peeled, seeded and diced
- ½ cup red split lentils
- 2 cups low salt vegetable stock

Directions

- Heat the coconut oil in a large saucepan; add the onion and sauté for about 5 minutes or until soft.

- Add the squash and cook for a further 5 minutes, stirring occasionally.

- Stir in the lentils and pour in the stock. Bring to a boil, cover, reduce heat and simmer for about 30 minutes until the squash is tender and the lentils soft.

Nutrition: The lentils in this recipe are an excellent source of complex carbohydrate and dietary fibre. In addition, they provide a good source of iron, protein and vitamin C.

Mixed Vegetables in Cheese Sauce

Ingredients

- 1 cup broccoli florets
- 1 cup cauliflower florets
- 1 carrot, peeled and diced
- ½ cup red pepper
- ½ cup frozen peas

Cheese Sauce

- 10g plain (all-purpose) flour
- 10g butter
- 1 cup whole milk, hot
- 45g grated Cheddar cheese

Directions

- Steam the broccoli, cauliflower, carrots, pepper and peas until tender.
- Purée to desired consistency.
- Mix with cheese sauce.

To Make the Cheese Sauce

- Melt the butter in a pan.
- Add the flour; stirring to form a paste (roux).
- Gradually add the milk, stirring until smooth.
- Simmer for 5 minutes, stirring constantly until mixture thickens.
- Remove from heat and stir in the grated cheese.

Nutrition: Cheese sauce is a great addition to your baby's diet. It tastes great plus it is a good source of calcium and has a high-fat content, which is important for growing babies.

Broccoli and Cauliflower Gratin

Ingredients

- 1½ cups broccoli florets
- 1½ cups cauliflower florets

Directions

- Steam the broccoli and cauliflower until tender.
- Purée in a blender.
- Mix in with cheese sauce (see previous page for cheese sauce).

Nutrition: This recipe will support your baby's liver and gut health and is also a good source of protein, calcium and folate.

Yummy Greens Purée

Ingredients

- 1 teaspoon unsalted butter
- ½ yellow onion, finely diced
- 1 cup courgette, trimmed and diced
- 1 cup broccoli florets
- 1 cup low salt vegetable stock
- ½ cup frozen peas

Directions

- Heat the butter in a saucepan. Add the onions and sauté until transparent.
- Add the courgette, peas and broccoli and cook for a few minutes.
- Add the vegetable stock, bring to a boil and simmer on a low heat for 10 minutes.
- Purée to desired consistency.

Nutrition: This purée is great for enhancing energy as it is a good source of iron, vitamins B6 and B12 as well as both soluble and insoluble fibre.

Sweet Potato, Spinach and Leek

The sautéed leeks add a milder, sweeter flavour than onions to this hearty sweet potato dish.

Ingredients

- 1 teaspoon butter

- 1 small leek (white and light green parts), chopped

- 1 sweet potato, peeled and diced

- Low salt chicken stock

- Handful (20g) of spinach, chopped

- ¼ cup grated cheese

Directions

- Melt the butter in a saucepan. Sauté the leek until softened.

- Add the sweet potato and enough chicken stock to just cover the vegetables. Bring to a boil, reduce the heat and simmer for 20 minutes until potatoes are soft. Add the spinach for the last 5 minutes of cooking.

- Remove from heat, drain cooking liquid and stir in the grated cheese.

- Place the ingredients in a blender and blend until smooth, adding a little of the cooking liquid to achieve desired consistency.

Nutrition: This well-balanced meal provides fat, protein and carbohydrate in the optimum proportions as well as a wide range of vitamins and minerals.

Ratatouille

This is one of Micah's favourite side dishes; he eats it with everything. Some of his favourite combinations are ratatouille with basmati rice, mashed potatoes, mashed plantain, spaghetti or boiled plantain.

Ingredients

- 1 tablespoon olive oil
- 1 small red onion
- 1 garlic clove, crushed
- 1 cup aubergine, peeled and chopped
- 1 cup courgette, peeled and chopped
- ½ cup red pepper
- ½ cup green pepper
- 400g tin chopped tomatoes

Directions

- Heat the oil in frying pan; add the onions and garlic. Cook, stirring for about 5 minutes until softened. Add the aubergine and courgette, stirring for about 5 minutes until the aubergine is browned slightly.

- Stir in the red and green peppers and cook gently for 10 minutes. Add the tomatoes and simmer, covered, for about 20 minutes until vegetables are tender. Purée in a food processor to desired consistency.

Nutrition: This immunity-boosting recipe is a great source of vitamin C, vitamin A and folate as well as dietary fibre and trace minerals.

Root Vegetable Purée

Ingredients

- 1 teaspoon unsalted butter
- ½ small onion, finely diced
- 1 sweet potato, peeled and finely diced
- 1 parsnip, peeled and finely diced
- 1 carrot, peeled and finely diced
- 2 cups water
- 1 low salt organic vegetable stock cube

Directions

- In a large pan, melt the butter then sauté the onion for 5 minutes, or until soft.

- Add the potatoes, parsnips, carrots, water and stock cube.

- Bring to a boil, reduce heat, cover and simmer for 15 to 20 minutes until the vegetables are tender.

- Allow to cool slightly then purée in a blender until smooth.

Nutrition: This energy-dense purée is great for hungry babies and provides complex carbohydrates as well as vitamins B1, B2, B6 and C.

Creamy Carrot, Broccoli and Cauliflower Purée

Ingredients

- 1 teaspoon coconut oil
- 1 small shallot, peeled and finely diced
- 1 carrot, peeled and finely diced
- 1 cup coconut milk
- 1 low salt organic vegetable stock cube
- 1 cup broccoli florets
- 1 cup cauliflower florets

Directions

- In a saucepan, heat the coconut oil and sauté the shallots until tender.
- Add the carrot, coconut milk and vegetable stock cube.
- Bring to a boil, reduce heat, cover and simmer for 15 minutes. Add the broccoli and cauliflower and simmer for a further 5 minutes until vegetables are soft.
- Allow to cool slightly then add the mixture to a blender. Purée to a lumpy consistency.

Nutrition: The coconut milk in this purée provides medium chain fatty acids, principally Lauric acid, which are similar to those found in human breast milk and scarcely found anywhere else in nature! Lauric acid can boost the immune system, improve digestion, and balance the blood sugar.

Watercress, Potato and Parsnip

Ingredients

- 1 teaspoon olive oil

- ½ small onion, chopped

- 1 cup potatoes, peeled and chopped

- 1 parsnip, peeled and chopped

- 1 cup low salt vegetable stock

- 2 bunches watercress, stemmed

Directions

- Melt the butter in a saucepan over a medium heat. Add the onions and sauté until the onion softens, about 5 minutes.

- Add the potato, parsnip and vegetable stock.

- Cover and simmer until vegetables are tender.

- Mix in the watercress; stir until watercress wilts (about 2 minutes).

- Purée in blender until smooth.

> Nutrition: This is a great recipe to support your baby's liver health and it provides a very good source of vitamins K, C and A as well as manganese.

My First Chicken Purée

A very tasty introduction to chicken, the sweetness of the sweet potato makes this dish more palatable for your baby.

Ingredients

- 1 cup diced chicken breast

- 1 small sweet potato, peeled and chopped

- 2 cups low salt chicken stock

Directions

- Place the chicken, sweet potato and stock in a pan. Bring to a boil and simmer gently for 20 minutes until the potato is soft and the chicken is cooked through.

- Purée in a blender, using some of the cooking liquid to get the desired consistency.

Nutrition: This is a blood-strengthening purée which provides a good source of protein, iron, vitamin C and folate.

Apricot Chicken

This recipe combines chicken with a fruit and it works! Combining meats with your baby's favourite fruits helps him to eat better and over time you can slowly reduce the amount of fruit or sweetness in his main meals.

Ingredients

- 1 tablespoon butter
- ½ small onion, peeled and chopped
- ¼ teaspoon ground cumin
- ¼ teaspoon ground coriander
- 1 cup diced chicken breast
- ½ cup dried apricots, chopped
- 1 small carrot, peeled and chopped
- 2 cups low salt chicken stock

Directions

- Melt butter in a saucepan; add the onion, ground cumin and ground coriander and sauté for 5 minutes until onions soften. Add the chicken and apricots and sauté for about 5 minutes. Add the carrots and pour over the chicken stock.

- Bring to a boil, then cover and simmer for about 25 minutes until the chicken is tender. Add more stock or water if it starts to dry out.

- Purée to desired consistency.

Nutrition: The apricots in this recipe provide high levels of iron as well as vitamin C, which helps your baby to absorb iron. This dish is also rich in vitamin A, folate and antioxidants.

Sweet Chicken Dinner

Chicken thighs are perfect for this recipe. They are succulent and packed with so much flavour.

Ingredients

- 2 boneless, skinless chicken thighs, chopped
- 1 apple, peeled, cored and diced
- 1 pear, peeled, cored and diced
- 2 cups low salt chicken stock

Directions

- Add the chicken and stock to a saucepan. Bring to a boil, then simmer covered for 25 minutes. Add apple and pear and simmer for a further 5 minutes.

- Purée to desired consistency.

Nutrition: This recipe is a good source of protein, iron and vitamin C as well as soluble and insoluble fibre to keep your baby's gut healthy.

Chicken, Broccoli and Butternut Squash

Ingredients

- 1 cup diced chicken breast
- 1 cup butternut squash
- 1 cup broccoli florets
- Low salt chicken stock

Directions

- Place chicken and butternut squash in a saucepan with the stock and cover. Simmer gently for 20 minutes.
- Add the broccoli and simmer for a further 5 minutes until the vegetables are tender. Purée to desired consistency adding a little of the cooking liquid.

Nutrition: This recipe is packed with the B vitamins required for energy as well as iron, vitamin C and protein.

Creamy Chicken

Although it has a higher fat content, occasionally serving your little one chicken with its skin on is acceptable as a growing baby needs the calories – not to mention chicken with skin on is juicier and yummy.

Ingredients

- 2 bone-in, skin-on chicken thighs
- 1 carrot, peeled and chopped
- 2 medium potatoes, peeled and chopped

Cheese Sauce

Refer to Mixed Vegetables in Cheese Sauce recipe.

Directions

- Add enough water to cover the chicken, carrot and potatoes; boil until tender. Shred the chicken, discarding the bones.
- Purée to desired consistency.
- Mix together with desired amount of cheese sauce.

Nutrition: This recipe provides a good source of calcium, potassium, protein and vitamins A and C, which make it blood-strengthening and immunity-boosting

Tasty Turkey Purée

Ingredients

- 1 cup boneless, skinless, turkey breast, diced
- 1 carrot, peeled and chopped
- ½ cup red pepper, deseeded and chopped
- 1 cup low salt chicken stock

Directions

- Put the turkey, carrot, pepper and stock in a saucepan and simmer for about 30 minutes until the vegetables are tender.

- Purée the mixture until it is of a consistency suitable for your baby.

Nutrition: Turkey is an excellent source of zinc, phosphorus, potassium and B vitamins as well as protein.

Sweet Beef Dinner

Ingredients

- 250g minced beef
- 2 cups low salt beef stock
- 2 apples, peeled, cored and diced

Directions

- Place the beef and stock in a medium saucepan. Bring to the boil and simmer for 25 minutes, uncovered, until beef is tender. Add more stock or water if it starts to dry out.
- Meanwhile, steam the apples for 5 minutes or until tender.
- Purée the cooked beef and steamed apples to a consistency suitable for baby.

Nutrition: Red meat provides the most absorbable form of iron for your baby and the vitamin C from the apples in this recipe will help your baby to use it for maximum benefit.

My First Cottage Pie

Ingredients

- 1 tablespoon butter
- 300g minced beef
- 1 carrot, peeled and chopped
- 2 potatoes, peeled and chopped
- ½ cup frozen peas
- ½ tablespoon tomato purée
- 2 cups low salt beef stock

Directions

- Melt the butter in a saucepan; add the beef, carrot, potatoes, peas and tomato purée. Pour over the stock, bring to the boil then simmer, covered, for 30 minutes.
- Purée to desired consistency.

Nutrition: This recipe is well balanced and provides a good source of zinc and iron. This is a good example of a recipe that uses many different coloured vegetables for maximum health benefit.

Nutrition: This recipe is rich in iron, protein, folate, vitamin A, vitamin C and the B complex. Your baby will also benefit from the antimicrobial properties of garlic.

Beef with Sweet Potato and Broccoli

Ingredients

- 1 tablespoon vegetable oil
- 1 garlic clove, minced
- 250g minced beef
- 1 cup sweet potato, peeled and finely diced
- 2 cups low salt beef stock
- ½ cup passata
- 1 cup broccoli florets, finely diced

Directions

- Heat the vegetable oil in a saucepan. Add the garlic and sauté until softened. Add the minced beef and fry for 5 minutes, or until browned.

- Add the diced sweet potato and passata. Pour in the stock to cover.

- Bring to the boil and then cover with a lid and simmer for 40 minutes.

- Add in the broccoli and continue to simmer for 10 minutes.

- For younger babies, purée the mixture. For older babies, purée the beef then mash the vegetables and mix together.

Veal with Vegetables

Ingredients

- 1 tablespoon coconut oil
- ½ small onion, chopped
- 1 garlic clove, minced
- 250g veal mince
- 1 carrot, peeled and diced
- 2 medium potatoes, peeled and diced
- 1 tablespoon tomato paste
- 1 low salt organic beef stock cube
- ¼ teaspoon curry powder
- Pinch of nutmeg
- 3 cups water

Directions

- Heat the coconut oil in a medium saucepan. Sauté the onions and garlic for 5 minutes. Add the veal mince, stirring for about 5 minutes. Add the carrots, potatoes, tomato paste, stock cube, curry powder, nutmeg and water and bring to the boil. Reduce heat and simmer, uncovered, for about 30 minutes or until the mixture has thickened.

- Purée the veal mixture with some of the cooking liquid to a texture appropriate for your baby.

Nutrition: Veal is an excellent source of vitamins A, C and B12 as well as folate. It is also very high in selenium, phosphorus and zinc, which are required for hormone production.

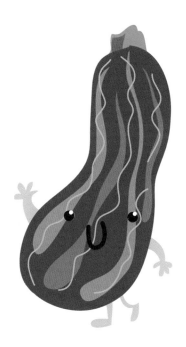

My First Fish Purée

This nutritious purée is so easy to prepare and your baby will love it.

Ingredients

- 1 fillet white fish (cod), deboned
- 1 cup milk
- 1 bay leaf

Directions

- Poach the cod in the milk with the bay leaf. Cover and simmer for 15 minutes. Discard bay leaf.
- Purée fish with a little milk to desired consistency.

Nutrition: Cod provides complete protein and is an excellent source of vitamin B12, iodine, selenium and phosphorus, which are required for hormone production.

Cod with Vegetables

Ingredients

- 1 teaspoon butter
- 1 carrot, peeled and chopped
- 1 medium sweet potato, peeled and chopped
- ½ medium red pepper, deseeded and chopped
- 1½ cups low salt vegetable stock
- 150g fillet of cod, chopped

Directions

- Melt butter in a saucepan. Add the carrot, sweet potato and pepper. Sauté the vegetables for 5 minutes. Add the vegetable stock. Bring to a boil and simmer for 15 minutes until the vegetables are tender, then add the cod and simmer for a further 10 minutes.

- Purée mixture to desired consistency.

> Nutrition: Cod provides complete protein and is an excellent source of vitamin B12, iodine, selenium and phosphorus. The vegetables in this meal provide complex carbohydrates, fibre and vitamins C, A, calcium and the B complex.

Salmon with Potato and Broccoli

- Ingredients

- 1 large potato, peeled and chopped

- 1 boneless salmon fillet, chopped

- ½ cup broccoli florets

- 1½ cups low salt vegetable stock

Directions

- Steam the potato until it is tender; mash. Meanwhile, simmer the salmon and broccoli in the vegetable stock for 10 minutes, or until the fish is cooked. Purée the fish and broccoli mixture.

- Mix the purée with the mashed potatoes; you can add some of the cooking liquid to thin the consistency.

Nutrition: Salmon is an excellent source of omega-3 fatty acids which are important for your baby's brain, eye and heart function. It is also a good source of protein, phosphorus, vitamin B6 and potassium.

Creamy Cauliflower and Plaice

Ingredients

- 1 cup cauliflower florets

- 2 cups milk

- 1 fillet plaice, deboned and chopped

- 1 bay leaf

- 30g Cheddar cheese, grated

Directions

- Steam the cauliflower until tender.

- Poach the fish in a saucepan with the milk and bay leaf for 10 minutes.

- Discard bay leaf and reserve the milk.

- For younger babies, purée the cauliflower, fish and cheese until smooth, adding a little of the reserved milk for desired consistency.

- For older babies, purée cauliflower and cheese with a little milk. Mash fish with a little milk and mix in with puréed cauliflower.

Nutrition: This recipe is a good source of calcium and protein as well as zinc, potassium and selenium, which support your baby's nervous system development.

Okra with Mackerel Soup

Mackerel is a delicious, nutritious fish packed with omega-3 fatty acids, which are great for a baby's brain development. I always try different okra recipes, but this was Micah's favourite at this stage. Ground dry crayfish is an essential ingredient in Nigerian cooking; I use it when making Nigerian soups and in some of my recipes for that traditional flavour.

Ingredients

- 3 mackerel fillets
- 2 cups water
- 1 low salt beef stock cube
- 1 small onion, chopped
- 2 ½ cups okra, finely chopped (for this weaning stage, you don't have to blend the okra)
- 1 tablespoon ground crayfish
- 1 tablespoon palm oil
- ½ cup chopped kale

Directions

- In a saucepan, add the fish, water, stock cube and onions. Bring to a boil and simmer for 7 minutes. Remove and carefully flake the fish (I always use my hand), removing any bones.

- Add the okra, ground crayfish and palm oil. Simmer uncovered, stirring occasionally for 10 minutes. Add kale and flaked mackerel. Cook uncovered for 5 more minutes.

Nutrition: This soup is an excellent source of omega-3 fatty acids and a good source of vitamins A, C and E, as well as folate. Okra has a mild laxative effect, which makes this soup useful for relieving constipation.

Ogbono with Mackerel Soup

Ogbono is a traditional Nigerian dish made with ground ogbono seeds. Like okra, babies love ogbono soup because of the gooey texture when cooked.

Ingredients

- 4 mackerel fillets
- 1 small onion, chopped
- 3 cups water
- 1 low salt beef stock cube
- 1 teaspoon Aromat seasoning
- 2 tablespoons palm oil
- ½ cup ground ogbono
- 1 tablespoon ground crayfish
- 1 cup chopped spinach

Directions

- In a saucepan, add mackerel fillets with the stock cube, Aromat seasoning, water, and half of the onion. Boil for 7 minutes. Carefully flake the fish (I always use my hand), removing any bones.

- In a separate saucepan, heat palm oil. Add remaining onions and sauté until translucent.

Add ogbono, using a cooking spoon to break up any lumps. Keep stirring to start the drawing process. Cook the ogbono, uncovered on a medium-low heat for 10 minutes, making sure to keep stirring.

- Gradually add the ogbono to the fish-stock mixture. Add crayfish. If the mixture is too thick, add some water, ¼ cup at a time. Season to taste.

- Add flaked mackerel and spinach. Let it cook, uncovered, for an additional 10 minutes or until the soup thickens.

Nutrition: Mackerel is a delicious, nutritious fish packed with omega-3 fatty acids, which are great for a baby's brain development.

My First Bolognese

Ingredients

- 1 tablespoon olive oil
- ½ small onion, finely chopped
- ½ celery stalk, chopped
- 1 garlic clove, minced
- 1 small carrot, peeled and finely chopped
- 250g minced beef
- 400g tin chopped tomatoes
- 1 tablespoon tomato purée
- Small amount of broken spaghetti to make desired quantity

Directions

- Heat the olive oil in a saucepan and add the onion, celery, carrot and garlic. Sauté for 5 minutes until the onion becomes translucent.

- Add the minced beef and brown, constantly chopping into it with a flat-edged wooden spoon to finely break it up.

- Add the chopped tomatoes and simmer for 45 minutes.

- Meanwhile, cook the spaghetti according to the manufacturer's instructions.

- Place everything in a blender and purée. It is OK if there are some lumps.

Nutrition: This recipe is a good source of protein, which your baby needs a lot of at this time of rapid growth. Bolognese also provides iron, vitamin C and the B complex, all of which are required for energy production.

Salmon Pasta

Ingredients

- 2 cups milk

- 1 garlic clove, whole

- 1 bay leaf

- 1 small salmon fillet, deboned

- 1 cup baby pasta shells

- ½ cup broccoli florets

- 30g Parmesan cheese, grated

- 1 tablespoon olive oil

Directions

- In a saucepan over a medium heat, bring the milk, garlic and bay leaf to a simmer.

- Add the salmon to the pan, bring back up to a simmer and poach the salmon for 10 minutes or until cooked.

- Remove the salmon from the milk, set aside and pour the milk into a bowl.

- Cook the baby pasta according to packaging instructions. If you have a steamer pan, steam the broccoli above the boiling pasta for 5 minutes. Alternatively, lightly simmer the broccoli in a pan of boiling water for 5 minutes.

- In a saucepan over a low heat add salmon, ½ cup of milk and broccoli.

- Stir in the cheese until melted, then add the pasta.

- Purée to the desired consistency.

Nutrition: A well-balanced meal that provides protein, fat and complex carbohydrates in the best proportions. Salmon is an excellent source of omega-3 fatty acids and broccoli provides vitamin C, folate and iron in good quantities.

Stage Two: Seven Months

	Breakfast (7am)	Mid-morning (9am)	Lunch (11.15/11.30am)	
Monday	Breastfeed or formula milk, Avocado and Cucumber Breakfast	Breastfeed or formula milk	Creamy Cauliflower and Potato, water	
Tuesday	Breastfeed or formula milk, Peach, Banana and Apple	Breastfeed or formula milk	My First Chicken Purée, yoghurt, water	
Wednesday	Breastfeed or formula milk, Ready Brek	Breastfeed or formula milk	My First Okra Soup[1], apple puree	
Thursday	Breastfeed or formula milk, Pear and Cinnamon Cereal	Breastfeed or formula milk	My First Fish Purée, water	
Friday	Breastfeed or formula milk, Avocado and Cucumber Breakfast	Breastfeed or formula milk	My First Okra Soup, apple puree	
Saturday	Breastfeed or formula milk, Peach, Banana and Apple	Breastfeed or formula milk	Sweet Beef Dinner, water	
Sunday	Breastfeed or formula milk, Ready Brek	Breastfeed or formula milk	My First Fish Purée, water	

[1]You can serve with traditional Nigerian sides such as eba, amala, semovita, tuwo shinkafa, plantain flour and semolina

Mid-afternoon (2.30pm)	Tea (5pm)	Bedtime (6.30pm)
Breastfeed or formula milk	Sweet Beef Dinner, water	Breastfeed or formula milk
Breastfeed or formula milk	Mashed plantain, grated pear, water	Breastfeed or formula milk
Breastfeed or formula milk	Sweet Beef Dinner, water	Breastfeed or formula milk
Breastfeed or formula milk	Lentils and Vegetables, water	Breastfeed or formula milk
Breastfeed or formula milk	Creamy Cauliflower and Potato, water	Breastfeed or formula milk
Breastfeed or formula milk	Yummy Greens Purée, yoghurt, water	Breastfeed or formula milk
Breastfeed or formula milk	Mixed Vegetables in Cheese Sauce	Breastfeed or formula milk

Stage Two: Eight Months

	Breakfast (7am)	Mid-morning (9am)	Lunch (11.15/11.30am)
Monday	Breastfeed or formula milk, Weetabix, grated pear	Breastfeed or formula milk	Cod with Vegetables, yoghurt, water
Tuesday	Breastfeed or formula milk, scrambled eggs, lightly buttered toast squares	Breastfeed or formula milk	My First Cottage Pie, water
Wednesday	Breastfeed or formula milk, Pear and Cinnamon Cereal	Breastfeed or formula milk	Sweet Chicken Dinner, water
Thursday	Breastfeed or formula milk, Ready Brek, yoghurt	Breastfeed or formula milk	Root Vegetable Purée, yoghurt, water
Friday	Breastfeed or formula milk, Weetabix, toast fingers	Breastfeed or formula milk	Mackerel and Ogbono Soup, yoghurt, water
Saturday	Breastfeed or formula milk, baby cereal, grated pear	Breastfeed or formula milk	My First Cottage Pie, mango slices, well-diluted juice
Sunday	Breastfeed or formula milk, Ready Brek, mashed banana	Breastfeed or formula milk	Penne with Vegetables, grated apple, water

Mid-afternoon (2.30pm)	Tea (5pm)	Bedtime (6.30pm)
Breastfeed or formula milk	Beet, Potato and Spinach Purée, water	Breastfeed or formula milk
Breastfeed or formula milk	Mackerel and Ogbono Soup, yoghurt, water	Breastfeed or formula milk
Breastfeed or formula milk	Penne with Vegetables	Breastfeed or formula milk
Breastfeed or formula milk	Cod with Vegetables, mashed avocado, water	Breastfeed or formula milk
Breastfeed or formula milk	Mixed Vegetables in Cheese Sauce, water	Breastfeed or formula milk
Breastfeed or formula milk	Beet, Potato and Spinach Purée, water	Breastfeed or formula milk
Breastfeed or formula milk	Sweet Chicken Dinner, water	Breastfeed or formula milk

Stage Two: Nine Months

	Breakfast (7am)	Mid-morning (9am)	Lunch (11.15/11.30am)	
Monday	Breastfeed or formula milk, omelette, toast fingers	Breastfeed or formula milk OR Drink of water plus a small piece of fruit	Butternut Squash and Lentils, grated pear, water	
Tuesday	Breastfeed or formula milk, Avocado and Cucumber Breakfast, yoghurt	Breastfeed or formula milk OR Drink of water plus a small piece of fruit	Beef with Sweet Potato and Broccoli, mango slices, water	
Wednesday	Breastfeed or formula milk, Weetabix, pear slices	Breastfeed or formula milk OR Drink of water plus a small piece of fruit	Okra with Mackerel Soup , yoghurt	
Thursday	Breastfeed or formula milk, Ready Brek, banana slices,	Breastfeed or formula milk OR Drink of water plus a small piece of fruit	Creamy Chicken, finely diced strawberries, water	
Friday	Breastfeed or formula milk, cheese on toast, baby cereal	Breastfeed or formula milk OR Drink of water plus a small piece of fruit	Ratatouille and mashed potatoes, water	
Saturday	Breastfeed or formula milk, Weetabix, yoghurt	Breastfeed or formula milk OR Drink of water plus a small piece of fruit	Mixed Vegetables in Cheese Sauce, grated apple, water	
Sunday	Breastfeed or formula milk, apple with baby cereal	Breastfeed or formula milk OR Drink of water plus a small piece of fruit	Butternut Squash and Lentils, grated pear, water	

Mid-afternoon (2.30pm)	Tea (5pm)	Bedtime (6.30pm)
Breastfeed or formula milk	Salmon Pasta, finely diced strawberries, water	Breastfeed or formula milk
Breastfeed or formula milk	Mixed Vegetables in Cheese Sauce, banana, water	Breastfeed or formula milk
Breastfeed or formula milk	Leek, Sweet Potato and Cauliflower, mango slices, water	Breastfeed or formula milk
Breastfeed or formula milk	Lentils with Vegetables, yoghurt, water	Breastfeed or formula milk
Breastfeed or formula milk	Salmon Pasta, finely diced strawberries, water	Breastfeed or formula milk
Breastfeed or formula milk	Beef with Sweet Potato and Broccoli, mango slices, water	Breastfeed or formula milk
Breastfeed or formula milk	Cheesy Cauliflower and Plaice, banana coins, water	Breastfeed or formula milk

CHAPTER EIGHT
WEANING STAGE THREE (TEN TO TWELVE MONTHS)

WEANING STAGE THREE

As your baby moves steps closer to family meals, this stage is all about continuing to explore new flavour combinations and textures. He should be enjoying finger foods and trying to self-feed with a spoon. To encourage self-feeding, let your baby hold a spoon when you are feeding him so he can start to learn to feed himself, while you have another spoon to do the actual feeding.

A lot of babies' tastes change regularly, so ensure you give her lots of variety in order to encourage healthy eating habits in the future.

As your baby gets older and begins to engage more with others around her, meal times should be seen as a social occasion. Try to eat one meal together as a family – we could not fit mealtimes in during the week when Micah was younger but on Saturdays we always ate breakfast together and brunch on Sundays.

Nutrition

Your baby is more active and adventurous than ever, so you need to give her a good balance of vitamins and minerals, as well as the proteins, carbohydrates and fats she needs to develop and the energy she needs for all her crawling or walking and exploring.

Offer a wide variety of foods – cereals and dairy at breakfast, protein, carbohydrates and vegetables for her main meals and fruit and dairy for dessert.

What to Feed Your Baby

Continue to avoid using honey or adding unnecessary salt or sugar to your child's meals. Maple syrup is preferable to caster sugar because it is nutrient-dense and low Glycemic Index (GI)

Until your baby becomes confident in chewing and swallowing food, avoid giving him whole grapes (I always cut grapes in half, lengthways, to avoid a choking hazard), whole nuts and olives or fruits with small seeds, as these pose potential choking hazards.

Make sure eggs are cooked through until both the white and yolk are solid.

He should still be drinking 500–600ml of milk (breast milk or formula milk), including the milk used in preparing his meals, until he is twelve months old.

Taste

At this stage, it is important to introduce your baby to more complex recipes that combine different flavours as well as herbs and spices.

If, like my family, your family enjoys spicy foods, you can also begin gently introducing these to your baby. Start with a mild curry and ground pepper, and use sparingly – much less than you would when preparing family meals. Gradually increase the amount only after you have established that your baby has no intolerances and is happy eating spicy food. Avoiding spicy food altogether will make it much more difficult to introduce these to him when he gets older.

Generally, toddlers dislike the flavour of fish, so the earlier you can train his taste buds to accept the flavour, the easier a time you will have later on. Try to incorporate strong-tasting fish like salmon into your child's diet. You can include it in his favourite meal. My son loves okra, so during this stage, we used salmon when preparing his okra and he gobbled it all up.

Food Texture

Continue to introduce more coarsely mashed, minced and chopped textures, as your aim is to gradually move your baby onto the same meals as the rest of the family. It will also help continue development of his jaw muscles and chewing skills. Finger foods will help in developing his hand and eye coordination. Finger foods should be easy to hold and gentle on the gums – do not worry if your baby has no teeth yet, it will surprise you how well he can chew with his gums!

You can encourage your baby's development of her fine motor skills by including finger foods at meal times. For example, you could give baby oats with some chopped fruit for breakfast, some pieces of vegetables with lunch or chopped fruits for dessert and mini sandwiches for dinner.

Remember that, although your child is becoming more independent, you should never leave her alone while she is eating.

Mixed Fruit Porridge

Ingredients

- 4 tablespoons of instant oats

- 1 cup whole milk

- ½ pear, peeled, cored and finely diced

- 2 strawberries, hulled and chopped

- 1 small banana, chopped

- A few drops of maple syrup (optional)

Directions

- Soak the oats for 30 minutes.

- Heat the milk in a small saucepan, add the pear, strawberries and oats and bring to a boil.

- Take off immediately and cover for about 5 minutes.

- Purée the porridge mixture in a blender.

- Stir in the chopped bananas and sprinkle with cinnamon.

- You can top with maple syrup.

Nutrition: This recipe provides calcium and vitamin D, which will help with the development of strong bones. It also contains potassium and is energy-dense without spiking your baby's blood sugar.

Nutrition: This recipe provides a good balance of protein and complex carbohydrate for your baby. Mango is a good source of vitamin C and provides enzymes to help with digestion.

Mango Muesli

Ingredients

- 4 tablespoons porridge oats
- 3 tablespoons creamy yoghurt
- ½ tablespoon maple syrup
- ¼ cup small, ripe mango, peeled, deseeded and finely diced

Directions

- Soak the oats in warm water for 30 minutes.
- Add the oats to the yoghurt and blend well.
- Mix the maple syrup and diced mango with the blended oats.

French Toast Squares

Ingredients

- 1 egg

- 2 tablespoons milk

- 1 teaspoon vanilla extract

- Pinch of cinnamon

- 1 tablespoon butter

- 2 individual slices sandwich bread

- Maple syrup to serve

Directions

- In a small bowl, beat the eggs a little, then add milk, vanilla extract and cinnamon. Beat mixture until well combined.

- Toss bread in egg mixture until the bread soaks up all the liquid.

- In a griddle or skillet, melt the butter over a medium heat. Fry bread squares, turning until all sides are lightly browned.

- Cut the French toast into squares and serve with maple syrup.

Nutrition: French toast is a good source of carbohydrates and saturated fat, which is great for growing babies. This recipe also provides calcium and vitamin D for strong bones and B vitamins for energy

Summer Fruit Compote

Ingredients

- 100g strawberries, hulled and diced

- 100g blueberries

- 100g raspberries

- Juice 1 orange

- 1 teaspoon maple syrup

- 1 vanilla pod

- Thick yoghurt to serve, optional

Directions

- Place all the fruits, vanilla pod and juice into a saucepan with maple syrup.

- Bring to a boil, then simmer for 3–5 minutes and use a wooden spoon to muddle and mash the fruit.

- Remove from heat and allow to cool to room temperature. Discard the vanilla pod. Serve with yoghurt.

Nutrition: This summer fruit compote is an antioxidant powerhouse and contains very impressive levels of vitamin C and vitamin K. The yoghurt provides good quality protein and the berries provide fibre. Maple syrup is preferable to caster sugar because it is nutrient-dense and low GI.

Fruit Salad Purée

Ingredients

- 2 cups strawberries, hulled and halved
- 1 cup sweet pineapple chunks
- 2 kiwi fruits, peeled and diced
- 1 teaspoon vanilla extract

Directions

- Combine strawberries, pineapple, kiwi and vanilla extract in a blender.
- Purée to a coarse texture.

Nutrition: This is a really high vitality purée which will support your baby's immune system and keep their skin soft and supple. It also provides enzymes that aid the digestion process.

Mixed Vegetable Omelette

Ingredients

- 1 teaspoon unsalted butter
- ½ small onion, diced
- 2 button mushrooms, finely chopped
- ¼ cup mixed red, green and yellow pepper
- 2 eggs, beaten
- Pinch of black pepper
- Aromat seasoning to taste

Directions

- Melt the butter in a saucepan.
- Add the onions, mushroom, peppers and black pepper to the frying pan. Sauté for 5 minutes or until the onion becomes translucent.
- Remove the sautéed vegetables and mix with the beaten egg. Season with pepper and Aromat to taste.
- Slowly stir the egg mixture back into the frying pan. Lightly brown one side, turn over and lightly brown the other side.

Nutrition: Omelettes are a really good option for babies and children because they are high in complete protein and vitamin D and you can add lots of vegetables. This recipe provides a rainbow variety of vegetables, which means your baby will get a range of health-promoting phytonutrients.

Simple Minestrone

Ingredients

- 1 tablespoon olive oil
- ½ red onion, finely diced
- 1 celery, trimmed and finely diced
- 1 garlic clove, minced
- 1 carrot, peeled and chopped
- ½ cup peeled and finely diced courgette
- 200g tin chopped tomatoes
- 1 tablespoon tomato puree
- 3 cups beef stock
- ¾ cup pasta shells
- Salt and pepper, to taste

Directions

- Heat olive oil in a medium saucepan over medium heat.
- Add onions and garlic. Sauté for 5 minutes.
- Add carrots and celery; season with salt and pepper, then cook for 3 additional minutes.
- Add tomatoes. Cover and bring to a boil. Reduce heat and simmer for 10 minutes.
- Pour in the stock, bring to a boil, and add pasta shells and courgette. Cook an additional 10 minutes or until pasta is cooked. Season to taste.

Nutrition: Soup is an easy and delicious way to get lots of vegetables into babies and young children. This recipe is high in fibre and complex carbohydrates and is a good warming winter option for the whole family.

Cheesy Potato Bake

Ingredients

- 500g potatoes, peeled and thinly sliced
- 1 tablespoon unsalted butter
- 1 garlic clove, minced
- 150ml full-fat milk
- 200ml double cream
- 50g Cheddar cheese
- 25g Parmesan cheese

Directions

- Preheat the oven to 180°C.

- In a medium saucepan, bring the water to a boil. Boil the potatoes for 2 minutes only to soften them, drain and set aside.

- Melt the butter in a saucepan and sauté the garlic for 5 minutes or until tender. Remove from heat. Slowly add the milk and cream stirring until combined. Return to heat and cook slowly until the sauce comes to a boil.

- Grease a medium baking dish with olive oil or butter.

- Arrange half of the potatoes, overlapping slightly, over the base of the dish, spoon half of the cheese sauce and sprinkle with half the Parmesan and half the Cheddar cheese. Place the remaining potatoes on top of the first layer, spoon over the remaining cheese sauce and sprinkle with the remaining cheese.

- Cover with foil and bake for 30 minutes or until potato is tender. Bake, uncovered, for a further 45 minutes or until the top is golden and potato is very tender.

Nutrition: This dish is classic comfort food and sure to be a hit with your baby! It is very energy-dense and provides a good balance of protein, complex carbohydrate and saturated fat.

Nutrition: This recipe is rich in the antioxidants beta-carotene and lutein, the carotenoids which give sweetcorn its distinctive colour. These are essential for developing good eyesight and preventing eye diseases. This recipe also provides calcium, B vitamins and vitamin C.

Kiddies' Sweetcorn Chowder

Ingredients

- 1 tablespoon coconut oil
- 1 tablespoon unsalted butter
- ½ stalk celery, trimmed and finely chopped
- 1 small yellow onion, peeled and finely diced
- ¼ teaspoon curry powder
- 1 tablespoon flour
- 200g potato, peeled and chopped into small cubes
- 1 cup vegetable stock
- 1 cup sweetcorn
- 1 cup full-fat cow's milk

Directions

- Heat the coconut oil with the butter in a saucepan over a medium heat. Once the butter has melted add the celery, onions, curry and thyme and sauté for 5 minutes or until softened.

- Sprinkle the flour over the celery and onions then add the potato. Sauté for 5 minutes stirring constantly.

- Add the stock, bring to a boil, and then reduce the heat to simmer for 5 minutes. Add the sweetcorn and cook for a further 5 minutes.

- Heat the milk to boiling point in a separate saucepan, then pour it over the vegetables and bring back to a boil over a low heat. Simmer for 15 minutes until the potatoes are tender.

- For younger babies you can mash the finished soup to the desired consistency.

- Serve with cheese on toast fingers.

Nutrition: This recipe is a good source of fibre and pre-biotics, which feed the beneficial bacteria in your baby's gut. It also provides protein and has antimicrobial properties to keep your baby's immune system strong.

Creamy Beans and Vegetable Porridge

Ingredients

- ½ onion, finely chopped
- 1 small carrot, peeled and diced
- ½ cup sweetcorn
- ½ tablespoon vegetable oil
- ½ teaspoon ground crayfish
- 1 cup dried black eyed beans
- ½ cup coconut milk
- 1 beef stock cube

Directions

- Place beans in a medium saucepan. Add enough water to cover the beans, bring to a boil and simmer on a medium heat. (A pressure cooker is advisable for cooking beans as it reduces cooking time considerably.)

- Cook the beans until tender, adding more water from time to time to avoid the beans drying up. You want to maintain the water at the same level as the beans to give them a porridge-like consistency.

- When the beans are soft but not mushy, add the crayfish, coconut milk, carrot, sweetcorn and stock cube. Simmer for 20–30 minutes until beans are very soft.

Okra with Mixed Vegetables

Kids love okra soup because of its gooey nature when cooked. It is one of the best first traditional soups for babies. Since kids love okra so much, I figured it's a great way to hide vegetables. I first tried this recipe on a fussy eater and he absolutely loved it. The important thing is to make sure the vegetables are finely diced and tender enough to be swallowed easily by babies.

Ingredients

- 1 teaspoon vegetable oil
- ¼ onion, peeled and chopped finely
- ½ carrot, peeled and finely diced
- 1 cup mixed red, yellow and green pepper, finely
- diced
- 2 mackerel fillet
- 1 salmon fillet
- 1 tablespoon palm oil
- 2 ½ cups of water
- Beef stock cube
- 2 cups of okra, chopped finely
- 1 tablespoon ground crayfish

Directions

- Heat the vegetable oil and sauté onions for 5 minutes. Add carrots and peppers and sauté for 5 more minutes.

- Add salmon, mackerel, palm oil, water, and stock cube. Cook for 10 minutes.

- Carefully flake the fish (I always use my hand), removing any bones. Mix in okra, flaked mackerel and salmon, and ground crayfish. Cook, uncovered, for an additional 10 minutes.

Nutrition: This recipe is a good source of vitamin A, vitamin C and the B vitamin complex, all of which play an important role in your baby's physical and mental development. Okra has a gentle laxative effect and therefore reduces the risk of constipation.

Ratatouille Baked Potatoes

Ingredients

Jacket Potatoes

- 1 russet potato per person
- 1 tablespoon olive oil

Ratatouille

Refer to Ratatouille recipe.

Directions

- Preheat the oven to 220°C.

- Wash the potatoes, dry and prick a few times with a fork. Pour some olive oil into your hands and rub over the potatoes.

- Place directly on the shelf in the oven and bake for 1¼–1½ hours until the skin is crisp and the flesh soft. Set aside.

- While the potatoes are baking, prepare the ratatouille.

- Cut a cross in the top of the potatoes and gently press on the ends to expose the flesh. Top with ratatouille.

> Nutrition: This recipe is a good source of vitamin C, vitamin A, potassium, folate and magnesium. Baked potatoes are an excellent source of dietary fibre and provide energy for your growing baby in the form of complex carbohydrate. Potatoes also contain a variety of phytonutrients that have antioxidant activity.

Plantain Pottage

My son loves plantain pottage: it is sweet, nutritious and since it's one-pot cooking, saves time in the kitchen as well. An all-round winner!

Ingredients

- 2 ripe plantains, cubed

- ½ cup chopped tomatoes in tomato sauce

- 1 tablespoon ground crayfish

- ½ cup of seafood or meat your child loves

- ½ onion chopped

- 2 tablespoons palm oil

- 1 beef stock cube

- Pinch of curry powder

- Pinch of ground nutmeg

- Handful of chopped kale and spinach leaves

Directions

- Add the cubed plantain to a saucepan. Add enough water to just cover the plantain, tomato, onion, meat or fish of your choice, curry, nutmeg and beef stock cube. Bring to a boil and simmer for about 15 minutes.

- Add the ground crayfish and oil, cook for 10 minutes. You can crush some of the plantain to help thicken the sauce.

- Add the kale and spinach leaves and turn off the heat after 5 minutes.

> Nutrition: This recipe is energy-dense and provides and a good source of protein and iron. It is also packed with B vitamins for energy and magnesium and potassium, which support nervous function

Nutrition: This recipe is packed with the B vitamins
required for energy, as well as iron, vitamin C and

Jollof Risotto

This is one of those meals where I threw everything together and it worked. The first time I made this meal, I was actually making a risotto but decided to add tomatoes last-minute to give a jollof twist (the Nigerian girl in me couldn't help it). It was such a hit and has been our go-to recipe for a long time now. It's a great way to introduce a new texture to little ones and encourages them to chew.

Ingredients

- 1 tablespoon olive oil
- 2 tablespoons finely diced onions
- ¼ cup carrot, peeled and finely diced
- ¼ cup red pepper, deseeded and finely diced
- ¼ cup courgette, finely diced
- ½ cup mushrooms, finely diced
- ½ cup blended tomatoes
- 1 tablespoon tomato purée
- 180g Arborio rice or basmati rice
- 4 cups chicken stock, plus extra if needed
- 15g butter
- 40g grated Parmesan cheese, plus extra to serve

Directions

- In a pan, heat olive oil then add the onions, courgette, mushroom and carrot. Sauté until tender.

- When the vegetables have softened, add rice, blended tomatoes and tomato purée. Turn up the heat and fry the rice mixture lightly for 1 minute.

- Reduce heat to medium low, then add half a cup of the stock, stirring occasionally, until it has all been absorbed by the rice. Continue adding and stirring a half cup of stock at a time until all the stock is used and the rice is plump and tender, which should take about 20–25 minutes.

- If the rice is not completely cooked, add a splash of more stock, and continue cooking until tender.

- Once the rice is soft enough to eat, remove the pan from the heat, then add butter and grated Parmesan. Cover and let stand for a few minutes.

- Serve in bowls, sprinkled with more grated Parmesan.

Nutrition: Cod is a low fat, flaky, white meat fish that is a good source of protein, phosphorus, niacin, and Vitamin B12. This recipe provides a good balance of protein, complex carbohydrate and colourful vegetables and tastes delicious.

Cod Stewed Potatoes

Ingredients

- 1 teaspoon butter

- 400g russet potatoes, peeled and cubed

- 2½ cups of water

- ¼ cup chopped tomatoes in tomato juice

- ½ cup deseeded and finely sliced mixed green, yellow and red peppers

- 100g cod fillet, cubed

- Beef stock cube, to taste

- Salt and pepper, to taste

Directions

- Melt the butter in a saucepan. Add the potatoes and sauté for 5 minutes.

- Add water to the potatoes. (If you want a thicker sauce, add less water.) Bring to a boil and simmer, uncovered, for 30 minutes.

- Add the chopped tomatoes and mixed peppers and continue simmering for another 20 minutes.

- Add the cod fillet, season with stock cube, salt and pepper, to taste and simmer for a further 10 minutes until the potatoes and vegetables are very tender.

- Let it stand for 15 minutes before serving.

Homemade Fish Fingers

Who doesn't love fish fingers? Not even a fussy eater can resist these delicious, homemade, healthy fish fingers – crunchy and crispy on the outside and soft and warm on the inside.

Ingredients

- Vegetable oil for frying
- 300g fillet of skinless, boneless white fish
- 1 cup breadcrumbs
- ¼ teaspoon garlic powder
- ¼ teaspoon dried herbs
- 1 teaspoon Aromat seasoning
- ¼ teaspoon black pepper (optional)
- 1 large egg, beaten
- 1 tablespoon milk

Directions

- Preheat the oil in a frying pan, over a medium heat.
- Dry the fillet with paper towels and cut into strips.
- Mix the breadcrumbs, garlic powder, dried herbs, Aromat seasoning and black pepper together.
- Get ready with 2 bowls or even plates, which are large enough for coating the strips.
- In the first bowl, crack an egg and whisk well. Add the milk to dilute the beaten egg.
- In the second bowl, pour your breadcrumb mixture.
- Dip each strip into the egg mixture and allow the excess egg to drip off.
- Coat the strip with the breadcrumb mixture. Slightly press the strip into the crumbs to make sure it is well coated. Let it stand for 5–10 minutes, this will help the coating stick to the strip better.
- Fry the fish in batches until crispy, about 6 minutes. Remove and drain on kitchen towels.
- Serve with sweet potato wedges, side vegetables and a sauce.

Nutrition: White fish such as cod promotes heart health because it is a good source of omega-3 fats and vitamin B12. It is also believed that regular fish consumption can help protect babies against childhood asthma. By making your own fish fingers you can select the best quality fish.

Cheesy Sole with Sweet Potatoes

Ingredients

- 1 sweet potato
- ½ cup chopped tinned tomatoes
- 1 teaspoon butter
- 45g grated Parmesan
- 100ml whole milk
- 1 sole or plaice fillet, deboned
- pinch of ground nutmeg, optional
- pinch of black pepper, optional

Directions

- Steam or boil the potato.
- Poach the fish in the milk until cooked. Set aside.
- Meanwhile, melt the butter in a saucepan, add the tomato and simmer for 10 minutes. Stir in the grated Parmesan.
- Mix the fish and sweet potato into the mixture. Sprinkle of pinch of ground nutmeg and black pepper. Mash to desired consistency.

Nutrition: This recipe packs a powerful nutritional punch. It provides lean protein and carbohydrate and sweet potatoes are one of the best sources of vitamin A. The milk and cheese provide calcium and the sweet potato provides over half of your baby's daily requirement of vitamin C.

Mini Fish Pie

Ingredients

- 550g potato, peeled and chopped
- 25g butter
- ½ cup hot milk
- 200g cod fillet, diced
- 1 tablespoon vegetable oil
- 1 garlic, minced
- 1 carrot, peeled and finely diced
- 50g frozen peas
- Handful of grated Cheddar cheese

Béchamel sauce:

- 30g unsalted butter
- 30g plain flour
- 1½ cups of warm milk
- pinch of nutmeg
- salt and pepper, to taste (optional)

Directions

- Preheat oven to 200°C.

- Boil potatoes in lightly-salted water for about 15 minutes, until soft. Mash with milk and butter. Lightly season with salt and pepper (optional)

- To make the béchamel sauce, melt butter in a pan. Add flour and stir to a paste. Gradually add milk, stirring, until mixture boils and thickens. Stir nutmeg into sauce and season with salt and pepper.

- Meanwhile, in another saucepan, heat vegetable oil. Add carrot, garlic, and peas. Cook for 5 minutes, until carrot softens.

- Transfer the sautéed vegetables into the béchamel sauce, then stir in the fish. Mix to evenly distribute the béchamel sauce. Spoon into ramekins.

- Spoon potato mash over the mixture in each ramekin until covered and sprinkle with Cheddar cheese.

- Bake in preheated oven for 20-25 minutes, or until the topping is crisp.

> Nutrition: The cod in this recipe provides complete protein and is an excellent source of vitamin B12, iodine, selenium and phosphorus, which are required for hormone production.

Chicken, Potato and Aubergine Goodness

This serves as a great introduction to the classic flavours of curry. My son loves curry, especially with basmati rice. It is also a great alternative to Nigerian stew and can be packed full of vegetable goodness.

Ingredients

- 2 tablespoons vegetable oil
- ½ onion, finely diced
- 1 garlic clove, finely diced
- 2 tablespoons curry powder
- 400g chicken thighs and legs
- 3 medium potatoes, peeled and diced
- 1 cup aubergine, diced
- 1 cup coconut milk
- 1 cup water
- 1 chicken stock cube
- Black pepper, to taste

Directions

- In a pot, heat the vegetable oil over medium heat. Add onions and garlic. Sauté for 5 minutes until the onions become translucent.

- Turn the heat to low, add the curry powder. Let it fry for 5 minutes. Be careful not to burn the curry.

- Add the chicken, sauté for 7 minutes.

- Add in the aubergine, potatoes, coconut milk, water and stock cube and bring it to the boil.

- Reduce the heat and simmer for 45 minutes until the chicken is very tender.

- When the curry is ready, take out the chicken thighs; using 2 forks, shred the chicken. For younger babies, you can purée the shredded chicken using a little of the cooking liquid to get the desired consistency. For older babies and toddlers, there is no need to purée.

- Mix the puréed or shredded chicken with the cooked potato and aubergine.

Nutrition: This recipe provides a good source of calcium, potassium, protein and vitamins A and C which make it blood-strengthening and immunity-boosting.

Nutrition: This soup provides fibre and excellent levels of
iron, vitamin A, vitamin C and the B vitamins. The chicken
thighs provide protein and calcium and add flavour.

Simple African Vegetable Soup

Ingredients

- 750g fresh spinach leaves
- 3 tablespoons palm oil
- 1 small onion, peeled and finely chopped
- 3 tomatoes
- 2 large sweet pointy pepper
- 1 garlic clove
- 1½ tablespoons ground crayfish
- 1 beef stock cube
- 3 chicken thighs

Directions

- In a saucepan, place the chicken, half of the onion and the stock cube. Add enough water to just cover the chicken. Bring to a boil and simmer for 30 minutes until the chicken is tender and the stock has thickened.

- Meanwhile, wash the spinach and chop into tiny pieces. Squeeze to drain out as much of the water as possible.

- Place the tomatoes, pointy pepper and garlic in a blender and purée to a smooth consistency.

- When the chicken is cooked, finely shred the meat and reserve the stock.

- In the same saucepan, heat the palm oil. Add the remaining onions and sauté for 5 minutes or until tender. Add the puréed tomato mixture to the palm oil and simmer on low heat for 15 minutes.

- Add the ground crayfish, spinach, chicken stock and shredded chicken, Season with Aromat seasoning to taste. Bring to a boil and let it simmer on medium low heat for 15 minutes until the spinach is very well cooked.

- Turn off the heat and let it stand for 5 minutes.

- Serve with amala or basmati rice.

Tasty Chicken Couscous

Ingredients

- 1 tablespoon unsalted butter

- ¼ small yellow onion, finely diced

- ½ cup carrot, peeled and diced

- ½ cup red pepper, deseeded and finely diced

- 2 cups chicken stock

- 1 cup couscous

- 1 cooked or grilled chicken thigh, finely shredded

Directions

- Melt the butter in a saucepan, then add the onions, carrot and pepper. Sauté for 5 minutes or until the onion softens.

- Add the shredded chicken and stock, bring it

to the boil and simmer for 10 minutes.

- Add the couscous, bring to the boil, then turn off the heat and leave it to rest for 5 minutes or until the couscous has absorbed all the water.

- Fluff up the chicken couscous using a fork.

> Nutrition: Couscous is a useful carbohydrate, which can bulk up simple meat and vegetable dishes like this one. If you use homemade chicken stock, you will significantly improve the mineral content and overall health benefits of this recipe.

Coconutty Turkey and Broccoli.

Ingredients

- 1 tablespoon coconut oil
- ¼ cup finely diced onion
- 1 garlic clove, minced
- ½ teaspoon ginger, finely chopped
- ½ teaspoon Aromat seasoning
- 250g minced turkey
- 1 cup crushed tomatoes
- 1 cup chicken stock
- ½ cup diced potatoes
- ½ cup coconut milk
- 75g broccoli, chopped into tiny florets
- Salt and pepper, to taste

Directions

- Heat oil in a saucepan. Add onions and garlic and sauté for 5 minutes. Add ginger, Aromat seasoning, and minced turkey. Brown turkey for 5 minutes, breaking up mince as the turkey cooks.

- Add potatoes, chopped tomatoes, chicken stock, and coconut milk. Simmer, uncovered, on medium-low heat for 20 minutes, or until potatoes are tender.

- Add broccoli, then season to taste with salt and pepper. Simmer, covered, for 7 minutes (or until broccoli is tender).

> Nutrition: This recipe is well-balanced in terms of protein and carbohydrate. Coconut is a good source of monounsaturated fats and also lauric acid, which is found in high concentrations in breast milk but scarcely anywhere else in nature.

Nutrition: This is a hearty and filling dish that will warm the whole family on cold nights. The recipe provides a good balance of protein, carbohydrate and fat. And, if you can use grass-fed beef, it is also a source of omega-3 fats. The vegetables provide vitamin C, beta-carotene, and manganese.

Beef Stew

This is one of the most delicious purées for babies.

Ingredients

- 1 tablespoon of unsalted butter
- ½ onion, finely chopped
- ¼ cup celery, diced
- 1 clove garlic, minced
- 250g stewing steak
- 2 tablespoons of cornflour
- 1 cup carrots, peeled and finely chopped
- 1 cup of butternut squash, peeled and diced
- 3 button mushrooms, finely chopped
- 1 cup sweet potato, peeled and finely chopped
- 450ml organic beef stock

Directions

- Preheat the oven to 180°C.
- Heat the butter in a casserole dish; add the onions, celery and garlic and fry for 5 minutes.
- In a sealable plastic bag, toss the beef in the cornflour, then add it to pan and brown for 5 minutes. Add the carrots, butternut squash, mushrooms, sweet potato and stock. Gently stir together.
- Cook in the preheated oven until the meat is tender. This can take anywhere between 2 and 3 hours.
- For younger babies (9 months and younger), purée all the meat and vegetables together to desired consistency. You can add some of the cooking liquid, a little at a time.
- For older babies (9 months and older) you want a lumpier texture. Purée all the beef with half of the vegetables. Leave other vegetables whole.
- Mix together.

Beef Fried Rice

This was one of my son's favourite meals; he could eat it every day and not get tired of it! The great thing about this recipe is that it's packed with lots of vegetables. It's also delicious and really quick to prepare.

Ingredients

- 1 tablespoon of butter
- ½ onion, chopped
- 1 garlic clove, minced
- 1 teaspoon fresh ginger, finely diced
- 150g minced beef
- 1 beef stock cube
- 1 carrot, peeled and chopped
- 1 cup mixed green, yellow and red peppers, finely diced
- ¼ cup sweetcorn
- ¼ cup finely diced green beans
- ½ teaspoon dried mixed herbs
- 2 teaspoons curry powder
- ½ teaspoon Aromat seasoning
- pinch of ground nutmeg
- 1½ cups of basmati rice
- 1 teaspoon olive oil

Directions

- Melt the butter in a pan over a medium-high heat. Add the onions, garlic and ginger. Fry, stirring until softened.

- Add the minced beef – don't cover the pan. Avoid over-stirring the mince as it fries. Allow the mince to develop a good brown colour before breaking it up and turning, then add the stock cube.

- Add the carrot and let it fry for a further 5 minutes.

- Add the rest of the vegetables, mixed herbs, nutmeg, Aromat seasoning and 1 teaspoon of curry powder. Pour in ¼ cup of water, bring to a boil, reduce the heat and let it simmer for 15 minutes or until vegetables are tender.

- Boil the rice with the remaining curry powder and olive oil.

- When the rice is cooked, add the desired quantity of beef and vegetable mix and let it simmer for a further 5 minutes.

Nutrition: This wonderfully balanced recipe provides good quality protein, essential fats and complex carbohydrate in the ideal proportions. Beef is a good source of iron and zinc, both of which are often lacking in infants' diets. This recipe also provides selenium, magnesium and zinc, all of which are essential for your baby's hormone production. The garlic and onions contain gut-friendly pre-biotics and the herbs provide B vitamins for energy.

Sweet Pork Dinner

Ingredients

- 1 small sweet potato, peeled and finely diced

- 1 centre-cut pork chop

- 1 teaspoon oil

- Pinch of black pepper (optional)

- 1 teaspoon butter

- 1 medium apple, peeled, cored and finely diced

- ½ small red onion, finely diced

- 1 cup chicken stock

Directions

- Steam the sweet potato until tender.

- Rub the pork chop with a little oil and season with pepper, if using. Heat a medium frying pan and fry the pork chop for 2 minutes on both sides. Dice the browned pork and discard bone; transfer to a plate.

- Melt the butter in the same saucepan and fry the apples and onions for 5 minutes or until the apples have softened.

- Pour in the stock and then return the pork to the pan and simmer for 10 minutes until the pork is cooked through. Mix in the sweet potato.

- Purée the mixture in a blender to a texture suitable for baby – at this stage you want to avoid giving your baby smooth purées.

Nutrition: Pork is loaded with various healthy vitamins and minerals, as well as high-quality protein. Therefore, unprocessed pork such as pork chops can make an excellent part of a healthy diet.

Beef with Lentils and Vegetables

Ingredients

- ½ tablespoon unsalted butter
- ½ small yellow onion, finely diced
- 1 garlic clove, minced
- 1 small carrot, peeled and finely diced
- 1 small celery stalk, trimmed and finely diced
- ½ cup red split lentils
- Pinch of ground nutmeg
- ¼ teaspoon curry powder
- 200g quality minced beef
- 1 beef stock cube
- 1 tablespoon tomato puree
- 3 ½ cups of beef stock

Directions

- Heat butter in a saucepan over medium heat.
- Add carrots, celery, garlic and onions. Sauté for 5 minutes, or until tender.
- Add minced beef, curry powder, nutmeg and beef stock cube. Brown beef while using a spoon to break it up.
- Add tomato paste and cook for 5 minutes. Then add lentils and 2 cups of water. Bring to a boil, then simmer and let it cook for 45 minutes. If the lentil mixture begins to dry out, add some water, ¼ cup at a time.
- Cool before serving.

Nutrition: This recipe is a good source of protein, which your baby's body requires at this time of rapid growth. Lentils provide iron, vitamin C and B complex, all of which are required for energy production.

Lamb Casserole

Ingredients

- 1 tablespoon olive oil
- 1 tablespoon plain flour, seasoned with salt and pepper
- 1 stick celery, trimmed and finely diced
- 1 garlic clove, minced
- 1 small yellow onion, peeled and finely diced
- 1 carrot, peeled and finely diced
- 1 sweet potato, peeled and finely diced
- 300g quality shoulders of lamb, boned
- 2 cups beef stock
- 220g tin of chopped tomatoes
- 1 tablespoon tomato paste
- 1 sprig fresh thyme

Directions

- Preheat the oven to 200°C.
- Finely dice the lamb. Place lamb and seasoned flour in a sealable bag. Shake to coat the meat evenly with flour.
- Heat half of the olive oil in a saucepan over medium-high heat. Cook lamb in batches, until browned. Transfer to a bowl.
- In the same saucepan, heat the remaining oil. Add garlic and onion, then sauté until the onion becomes translucent. Add carrots, celery and sweet potato. Season with salt and pepper. Add tomato puree and cook for 2 minutes.
- Pour in the stock, lamb, and chopped tomatoes. Bring to a boil, then transfer to a casserole dish and add thyme. Season to taste, then cover and cook in oven for 2–2½ hours, or until tender. Remove lid for the final half hour of cooking.

Nutrition: This stew is hearty and comforting. The lamb provides zinc and iron, which are sometimes difficult nutrients to get in sufficient quantities. The vegetables in this dish provide fibre, pre-biotics and many vitamins. Delicious!

Nutrition: The carrots add fibre and vitamins to an otherwise heavy dish. This dish is pure comfort food and will be loved by kids of any age.

Hidden Carrot Mac and Cheese

Ingredients

- 1 cup dried macaroni
- 2 small carrots, peeled and chopped
- 1 tablespoon butter
- 1 tablespoon plain flour
- 1 cup whole milk
- ½ cup grated cheese

Directions

- Cook the macaroni until soft. Drain and set aside.
- Cook or steam carrots until soft.
- Blend the carrots to a smooth consistency.
- In a pan, melt the butter. Add the flour and stir to a paste. Keep stirring as you gradually add the milk. Cook until the sauce begins to thicken, then add the cheese.
- Add the carrot mixture and fold the cooked, drained macaroni into the sauce until coated.

Cheesy Salmon Pasta

This recipe is rich and creamy, just what a growing, active baby needs.

Ingredients

- 1 cup pasta shells
- 75g salmon fillet
- ½ cup broccoli florets
- cup grated Parmesan
- Milk (enough to cover the salmon)
- ½ cup carrot, diced
- ½ cup cauliflower florets
- 15g butter
- 1 bay leaf

Directions

- Cook the pasta according to packaging instructions. (You can steam the broccoli above the boiling pasta.)

- In a saucepan over a medium heat, bring the milk and bay leaf to a simmer.

- Add the salmon to the pan, and bring back up to a simmer, poaching the salmon for 10 minutes. Flake the salmon, reserving the poaching liquid.

- Meanwhile, melt the butter in a saucepan. On a medium-low heat, sauté the carrots for 7 minutes. Add broccoli and cauliflower. Sauté until the broccoli is soft.

- Add the flaked salmon and pasta to the carrot mixture. Add in ½ cup of the poaching milk to the mixture. Simmer for 3 minutes.

- Take off heat and stir in the grated cheese.

Nutrition: This recipe is a good source of vitamin K, which your baby needs for proper blood clotting. It also provides vitamin B6, iron, folate, and vitamin C, all of which are required for maintaining strong blood and a healthy immune system. The salmon provides omega-3 fatty acids for optimum brain development.

Macaroni Carbonara

Ingredients

- 1¼ cups elbow macaroni
- 20g tablespoon butter
- 1 garlic clove, crushed
- 4 slices of prosciutto, finely chopped
- 2 eggs
- 50g Parmesan cheese, grated
- Pinch of black pepper

Directions

- Cook the macaroni according to packaging instructions.

- Meanwhile, melt the butter in a saucepan over a medium-low heat, toss in the garlic and prosciutto and sauté until the prosciutto is golden brown.

- Beat the eggs in a medium-size bowl, mix in the cheese with the beaten eggs, stirring well to prevent lumps. Season with a pinch of black pepper and set aside.

- When the macaroni is cooked, add the hot, drained macaroni (when you drain, leave the macaroni a little moist, this will help to thin out the sauce so it coats all the pasta) to the pan and stir for 2 minutes. Remove the saucepan from the heat and pour the egg/cheese mixture into the macaroni, keep stirring until the macaroni is thoroughly coated.

Nutrition: This recipe provides a good balance of carbohydrate and quality protein as well as calcium and vitamin D, which your baby needs to build strong bones.

Stage Three: Ten to Twelve Months

	Breakfast (7am)	Mid-morning (9.30am)	Lunch (11.30am/12.00pm)	
Monday	Mango Muesli, lightly buttered toast fingers, breastfeed or formula milk	Milk OR Drink of water plus a small piece of fruit	Okra with Mixed Vegetables, fruit, water	
Tuesday	French Toast Squares, Peach, Banana and Apple, breastfeed or formula milk	Milk OR Drink of water plus a small piece of fruit	Hidden Carrot Mac n Cheese, pear slices, water	
Wednesday	Scrambled eggs with lightly buttered toast fingers, breastfeed or formula milk	Milk OR Drink of water plus a small piece of fruit	Cod Stewed Potatoes, yoghurt, water	
Thursday	Weetabix, yoghurt with fruits, breastfeed or formula milk	Milk OR Drink of water plus a small piece of fruit	Beef Fried Rice, finely diced strawberries, water	
Friday	Lightly Buttered Toast Fingers, Summer Fruit Compote, breastfeed or formula milk	Milk OR Drink of water plus a small piece of fruit	Tasty Chicken Couscous, water	
Saturday	Mashed avocado on toast, Fruit Salad Purée, breastfeed or formula milk	Milk OR Drink of water plus a small piece of fruit	Okra with Mixed Vegetables, fruit, water	
Sunday	Mixed Vegetable Omelette, toast fingers, breastfeed or formula milk	Drink of water plus finely diced vegetables, fruits or finger foods	Hidden Carrot Mac n Cheese, pear slices, water	

Mid-afternoon (2.30pm)	Tea (5pm)	Bedtime (6.30pm)
Breastfeed or formula milk	Jollof Risotto, yoghurt, water	Breastfeed or formula milk
Breastfeed or formula milk	Plantain Pottage, diced papaya, water	Breastfeed or formula milk
Breastfeed or formula milk	Simple Minestrone, water	Breastfeed or formula milk
Breastfeed or formula milk	Sweetcorn Chowder, pear slices, water	Breastfeed or formula milk
Breastfeed or formula milk	Cheesy Salmon Pasta, water	Breastfeed or formula milk
Breastfeed or formula milk	Plantain Pottage, diced papaya, water	Breastfeed or formula milk
Breastfeed or formula milk	Selection of mini sandwiches, yoghurt, water	Breastfeed or formula milk

CHAPTER NINE

TODDLERS AND BEYOND

(FROM TWELVE MONTHS UPWARDS)

TODDLERS AND BEYOND

By now, your toddler is old enough to join the rest of the family at mealtimes. Eating together, whether eating at home or eating out, is perfect for some extra family bonding time even if she cannot have the same food as you.

Most parents may find that after eating enthusiastically as a baby, your toddler's eating will suddenly become cautious, fussy and fickle. It is normal for toddlers to be less interested in food than they were as babies. Bearing this in mind, try not to get anxious about mealtimes; the truth is most toddlers will eat enough to keep them going even when they are refusing food at times. There are useful tips for dealing with fussy eaters, starting on page 34. However, if you are really worried about what your toddler eats, keep a food chart for a week and write down her food intake.

Nutrition

At this age, your child is growing very quickly and is very active, so he needs plenty of energy and nutrients. A healthy and varied diet should provide all the nutrients your toddler needs. Aim to give your toddler three nourishing meals a day, and two healthy finger food snacks in between.

Snacks and Treats

Young children need some fat in their diets for energy and growth, but it's important not to have high-fat and high-sugar foods (e.g., chips, lollipops and ice cream) every day. Children who eat "treat" foods too often tend to eat less healthy food. Sweet foods can also cause holes in teeth. You can help stop your toddler developing a sweet tooth by limiting how often you give sweet food or drinks to your child. Instead of avoiding high-fat and high-sugar foods and talking about them as "bad" foods, teach your child to enjoy them as an occasional treat.

Try to offer snacks and treats well before mealtimes so your child has time to get hungry again.

Drinks

Even though your little one is now eating more grown-up food, milk matters. Of course the amount he is drinking will have decreased but your toddler still needs between 350ml and 500ml of milk a day. At this stage you can offer full-fat cow's milk.

Fully skimmed and 1% fat milk aren't suitable as a main drink until your child is five years old because they don't contain enough vitamin A and skimmed milk doesn't contain enough calories.

It is a good idea to give vitamin drops to children under five, particularly vitamins A, C and D. Check with your GP or healthcare provider.

Try to avoid giving your toddler a lot of milk in the hour before a meal as it will fill her up. If she is thirsty, give her a drink of water instead.

Try not to give your toddler fizzy, sugary drinks and fruit squash because fruit juices are acidic and contain quite a lot of natural sugar, which can cause tooth decay. They can also fill children up so they don't eat enough food to get all the nutrients they need. If you do give these drinks, restrict them to meal times only, and dilute juices with water (ten parts water to one part juice). Diluting them and drinking them with meals can help minimise the damage they do to your toddler's teeth.

If you haven't already, try to phase out bottles so that all your toddler's drinks, including milk, are given in cups or beakers.

Foods to Avoid

Don't give raw eggs, or food that contains raw or partly cooked eggs, to your toddler because of the risk of salmonella, a type of food poisoning. If you give eggs to your toddler, make sure the eggs are cooked until both the white and the yolk are solid.

Don't give whole peanuts or any type of whole nuts to children under five years old because they could cause choking. It's a good idea always to grind nuts finely.

Avoid shark, swordfish and marlin because the high levels of mercury in these fish can affect a child's developing nervous system.

You might want to avoid raw shellfish to reduce the risk of food poisoning.

Fruitilicious Oatmeal

Prep this the night before so the oats can absorb the moisture in the milk, leaving a pudding consistency. It's a yummy, healthy breakfast the whole family can enjoy together.

Ingredients

- ½ cup rolled oats
- ½ cup whole milk
- Greek yogurt to serve
- ½ cup mixed berries, mashed
- Maple syrup to serve

Nutrition: By soaking the oats overnight you effectively begin the digestion process for your baby, which makes the nutrients much more easily accessible. Berries are packed with antioxidants and vitamin , both of which support immune function.

Directions

- Before bed, mix together oats and milk; place them in a sealed container and refrigerate overnight.
- In the morning, add a drizzle of maple syrup and top with a layer of Greek yogurt and mixed berries.

Nutrition: This smoothie is a good source of calcium and potassium, which are needed to strengthen your baby's growing bones. It also provides excellent amounts of vitamin C, vitamin B6 and manganese.

Breakfast Smoothie

Smoothies are a great way to give your kids the nutrient-rich fruits and veggies their little bodies need. Mix your child's favourite fruits with yoghurt for a yummy breakfast treat.

Ingredients

- 1 frozen, ripe banana, sliced
- 1 tablespoon honey
- ½ cup Greek yoghurt
- 300g frozen strawberries
- ½ cup whole milk
- Pinch of cinnamon

Directions

- Place the banana, yoghurt, honey, strawberries and milk in a blender.
- Purée until smooth and fruity.
- Top with a pinch of cinnamon.

Easy, Yummy Pancakes

Ingredients

- 1 cup plain flour
- 1 tablespoon sugar
- 2 eggs
- 375ml whole milk
- ½ cup melted butter
- Maple syrup to serve, optional

Directions

- Sift the flour and sugar into a large mixing bowl. Make a well in the centre of the bowl and break the eggs into it. Beat in the egg and then milk a little at a time until batter is smooth and lump free.

- Spoon 2 tablespoons of butter into the batter and whisk it in.

- Set a frying pan or flat grill pan over a medium heat and carefully lubricate it with some buttered kitchen paper. When hot, cook your pancakes for 1 min on each side until golden, keeping them warm in a low oven as you go.

Nutrition: This simple recipe provides a balance of protein and carbohydrate. Serve with fresh fruit and yoghurt for a more nutrient-dense breakfast.

Nigerian Egg Stew

This is a weekend breakfast staple for many Nigerian families. It is easy to prepare and delicious. It is mostly eaten with boiled yam, but I find yam too heavy for young kids. You can substitute boiled yams with boiled sweet potatoes or boiled plantain.

Ingredients

- 2 tablespoons vegetable oil
- ½ small yellow onion, diced
- 2 tomatoes, finely diced
- ¼ teaspoon curry powder
- Pinch of ground nutmeg
- ¼ teaspoon dried thyme
- Pinch of salt
- ½ teaspoon of Aromat seasoning
- 2 eggs

Directions

- Heat the oil in a saucepan; add the onion and sauté for 5 minutes until tender.

- Add the tomatoes, curry powder, nutmeg, thyme and salt. Simmer on a low heat for 10 minutes.

- Crack the eggs into a bowl and whisk. Pour into tomato mixture and stir gently to mix all ingredients together. Simmer for one minute.

- Serve with boiled sweet potatoes or fried plantain.

Nutrition: This recipe provides significant amounts of bonestrengthening vitamin K, and lycopene, an antioxidant which may also support bone health. It is a good source of vitamin C and provides antimicrobial properties and insoluble fibre to support your baby's digestion.

Breakfast Semolina

Ingredients

- 1 cup milk

- ½ tablespoon maple syrup

- ¼ cup semolina

- ½ banana, sliced into coins

- 1 teaspoon seedless berry jam, melted

- Pinch of cinnamon

Directions

- Heat the milk and maple syrup in a saucepan.

- Gradually add the semolina, stirring until you achieve your desired consistency. Usually about 5 minutes.

- Decorate the top with the sliced banana, seedless berry jam and sprinkle of cinnamon.

Nutrition: Semolina is a good source of complex carbohydrate, which your baby requires for energy and growth. It also provides vitamin E, which supports the immune system and skin health and many trace minerals.

Nutrition: Plantain is energy-dense and provides good
levels of vitamin C, B vitamins and potassium, all of
which support hormone production. The vegetables in
this recipe provide fibre and a range of immune system-
supporting phytonutrients.

Plantain Frittata

Ingredients

- 1 ripe plantain, peeled and diced
- Vegetable oil, for frying
- ½ teaspoon salt
- 1 teaspoon Aromat seasoning
- Pinch of nutmeg
- 1 medium yellow onion, diced
- ½ cup mushrooms, finely diced
- ½ red pepper, finely diced
- ½ yellow pepper, finely diced
- 6 eggs
- 1 cup broccoli florets

Directions

- Preheat oven to 180°C.
- Deep-fry the plantain in the vegetable oil until golden brown.
- Cook the broccoli florets in boiling water for 3 minutes. Drain and plunge into cold water; drain broccoli well and set aside.
- Heat the oil over medium heat and sauté the peppers for 7 minutes until they start to soften, Add the broccoli; sauté for 2 minutes.
- Meanwhile, whisk the eggs, salt, Aromat and nutmeg in a medium size bowl.
- Once the vegetables are soft, add the plantain and vegetable mixture to the egg mixture, then pour it into the pan. Cook over a fairly low heat for 10–15 minutes, until the egg is starting to set up on top – do not stir.
- While the eggs are cooking, preheat the grill.
- Transfer the pan and grill until the frittata is nice and brown on top, about 3–5 minutes. Remove and let sit for 5 minutes before cutting into wedges.

Apple and Pear Compote

This compote can be served for breakfast or dessert. You can serve with vanilla ice cream or vanilla custard for a yummy dessert or natural yoghurt or muesli for breakfast.

Nutrition: This recipe is rich in potassium, which your baby needs to break down and use carbohydrate and to build muscle. The fruits in this recipe also provide trace minerals, vitamin C and fibre.

Ingredients

- 3 delicious apples, peeled and diced
- 2 pears, peeled and diced
- 1 tablespoon maple syrup
- ¼ cup water
- Pinch of cinnamon
- Pinch of nutmeg

Directions

- Add the apples, pears, water, maple syrup, cinnamon and nutmeg to a saucepan, bring to a boil and simmer for 10–12 minutes until apples and pears are very tender and juices are thickened to a thin syrup.
- Set aside for 15 minutes to cool slightly then serve.
- You can store in the fridge, in an airtight container for up to 3 days.

Grilled Pineapple Pops

Grilled pineapple is so simple and a yummy dessert for kids.

Ingredients

1 cup ripe pineapple, peeled and cut into bite-size cubes

½ cup maple syrup

Directions

- Place pineapples in a sealable plastic bag and add maple syrup. Marinate for a minimum of 30 minutes.

- Preheat a greased chargrill or large non-stick frying pan over medium heat.

- Place coated pineapple cubes into hot pan/grill. Allow pineapple to caramelise on all sides, turning every few minutes and watching carefully so as not to burn.

- Drizzle with excess caramelised juices from pan. You can serve with homemade ice cream or Greek yoghurt.

Nutrition: A portion of pineapple provides more than your baby's daily requirement of vitamin C, which is a great infection fighter and collagen synthesiser.

Nutrition: Chocolate is high in sugar and should definitely be reserved as an occasional treat. By serving chocolate with fruit it goes much further and your baby gets the benefit of vitamins and fibre from the fruit.

Chocolate Dipped Fresh Fruits

Most kids love chocolate; combine it with fruits and you have a winner. This is a great way to get your kids eating more fruits for dessert. The best part about this dessert is it takes just a few minutes to make and it tastes heavenly with virtually no effort at all. I have to warn you, though, this dessert is addictive. Micah loves it so much!! You can use your favourite kind of chocolate for this dip – I have used dark, milk and white chocolate and Micah loved all three!

Ingredients

- 1 large mandarin/tangerine/clementine, peeled and segmented
- 1 kiwi fruit, peeled, halved and cut into 1cm slices
- 4 large strawberries, hulled and halved
- 1 ripe pear, quartered lengthwise, cored and cut into wedges
- Spices, optional. The following spices are delicious with chocolate: cardamom, cinnamon, nutmeg, pumpkin spice.
- 1 tablespoon of butter
- 200g milk chocolate or your chocolate of choice

Directions

- Melt chocolate and butter in a heatproof bowl over a pan of simmering water. Pour warm chocolate into small serving bowls for dipping.
- Arrange fruits on a serving plate. Serve with chocolate dip.

Nutrition: This recipe is high in fibre and low in fat, which is not what you would usually expect from ice cream! The berries are packed with antioxidants and vitamin C and the banana provides potassium and complex carbohydrate.

Blueberry Banana Ice cream

To make the ice cream for this yummy dessert, you need only one ingredient – and no ice cream maker! That's right, you read right. All you need is a banana – no additional dairy, sweeteners or ingredients needed for this ice cream dessert. Mix in some berries and you will have the kids asking for more… Don't tell them your secret though!

Ingredients

- 5 large, ripe bananas (bananas should be soft with brown spots)
- 1 cup blackberries, frozen
- 1 teaspoon pure vanilla extract
- Coconut flakes for serving

Directions

- Peel the bananas and cut into evenly sized coins.
- Put the bananas in an airtight container or freezer bag and freeze for at least 5 hours, ideally overnight.
- Blend the frozen bananas and blueberry in a small food processor. Keep blending, scraping the sides of the processor until the mixture is smooth and creamy like soft-serve ice cream texture.
- If you want it harder, transfer back into airtight container and freeze it until solid like traditional ice cream.
- Spoon ice cream into bowls, top it off with coconut flakes and serve immediately.

Mixed Fruit Parfait

If you are looking for a delicious, healthy dessert that doesn't have a mountain of sugar then this is a perfect recipe. It will please even the pickiest palette and encourage more fruit consumption! Keep your child's favourite fruits in mind and add a little tempting topping to sweeten the deal. This mixed fruit parfait is a great way to let kids help in the kitchen. It also exposes them to different types of food. Kids will enjoy measuring the yoghurt and spooning it into the dish. Allow kids to choose different fruits to top their yoghurt sundaes such as raisins, peaches, or bananas.

Ingredients

- Thick natural yoghurt

- Ice cream wafers

- Bananas, cut into coins

- Strawberries, hulled and halved

- Kiwi, peeled and halved

- Whipped cream for topping

- Sprinkles (optional)

Directions

- Combine the strawberries, bananas, and kiwi in a bowl. In sundae glasses, layer fruit mixture and yoghurt alternately until you fill the glasses. Top with whipped cream and sprinkles and serve.

Nutrition: This recipe is an excellent source of protein, calcium, and probiotics, which are microorganisms that help keep your baby's digestive system working properly. The fruits add a vitamin-rich and naturally sweet flavour to the parfait.

Nutrition: Homemade Fruitsicles are a much healthier option than store-bought versions as you avoid the additives, artificial sweeteners and excess sugar content. The recipes below are nutrient-dense and taste delicious so your baby can enjoy regular treats without you having to worry.

Mango and Yoghurt Popsicle

Ingredients

Mango Purée

- 2½ cups mango chunks, fresh or frozen
- 1 cup pineapple juice

Yoghurt Purée

- 1 cup Greek yoghurt
- 3 tablespoons maple syrup
- 5 tablespoons water
- ½ teaspoon vanilla extract

Directions

- In a blender or food processor, purée the mango chunks with the pineapple juice until smooth. Transfer to a bowl and set aside.

- In another bowl, combine yoghurt, maple syrup, water and vanilla extract. Stir until homogeneous.

- Pour mango purée about ¼ of the way into each popsicle mould. Place in freezer for 45 minutes until almost solid.

- Remove the mould from the freezer; pour yoghurt mixture to fill half of the remaining space in the mould. Put in the popsicle sticks. Place in freezer for 1 hour.

- Pour remaining mango purée into moulds until liquid reaches the top of the mould. And place back into the freezer until the pops are completely frozen, usually 5–6 hours.

Watermelon and Coconut Popsicle

Ingredients

- 2 cups puréed watermelon
- Organic coconut milk
- 2 tablespoons honey
- 3 tablespoons water

Directions

- Pour the blended watermelon about 2/3 of the way into the popsicle mould. Secure the lid to the mould and insert popsicle sticks. Freeze for 2 hours.

- Shake coconut milk thoroughly to mix. Pour out 1/2 cup of coconut milk and mix with honey and water.

- Remove the lid from the popsicle mould and fill the moulds to the top with coconut milk.

- Place back into the freezer and freeze for at least 5–6 hours before eating.

- Run popsicle mould under warm water, pop popsicle out of mould and serve.

Rainbow Popsicle

Ingredients

- 1 cup puréed ripe mango
- 1 cup puréed strawberries
- 1 cup puréed blackberry
- 1 cup puréed kiwi

Directions

- Pour mango, strawberry, blackberry and kiwi purée to each fill up ¼ of the popsicle mould. You can go in any order to create a colourful popsicle. I like to start with mango, then strawberry, then kiwi and finally blackberry.

- Put in your popsicle stick and freeze for a minimum of 6 hours.

Strawberry Banana Popsicle

Ingredients

- 1 cup strawberries, frozen
- 1 banana, frozen
- ½ cup vanilla yoghurt
- ½ cup milk
- 1 tablespoon honey or sugar

Instructions

- Add all of your ingredients in a blender and process until smooth. Pour mixture into popsicle mould.
- Place in the freezer and freeze for at least 5–6 hours before eating.

Potato Pottage

Ingredients

- 3 cups peeled and diced potatoes
- 2 sweet pointed peppers (tatashe)
- 1 red chilli (optional)
- 2 tomatoes
- 2 garlic cloves
- ½ teaspoon fresh ginger
- 2 tablespoons palm oil
- 1 small onion, finely diced
- 1 tablespoon ground crayfish
- 1 mackerel fillet
- 1 beef stock cube
- 1 small lemongrass stalk
- 1½ cups beef stock
- ½ teaspoon curry powder
- Salt, to taste
- Handful of chopped kale or spinach leaves

Directions

- Blend peppers, chilli, tomatoes, garlic and ginger until smooth.

- Heat palm oil in a saucepan over medium heat; sauté onion until tender and fragrant.

- Pour the blended tomato mixture in a saucepan, bring to a boil, and then simmer on medium heat for 10-15 minutes, until the tomato mixture reduces significantly. Stir occasionally to prevent burning.

- Add 2 cups of stock, ground crayfish, stock cube, lemongrass and curry powder. Salt to taste, if necessary. Bring to a boil and simmer another 5 minutes.

- Meanwhile add potatoes to a saucepan, cover with cold water, and then bring to a boil. Boil for 5 minutes (to soften but not cook them). Drain potatoes.

- Transfer potatoes to the tomato mixture and simmer for 15 minutes on medium-low heat until the potatoes are tender. Add the mackerel fillet and simmer for an additional 15 minutes, breaking up when mackerel is cooked.

- Add the kale or spinach leaves, mash ¼ of the potatoes, and cook for 5 more minutes. Discard the lemongrass stalk before serving.

Nutrition: White fish provides complete protein and is an excellent source of vitamin B12, iodine, selenium and phosphorus, which are required for hormone production.

Cauliflower Gratin

Ingredients

- 750g cauliflower, broken into florets
- 40g butter
- 40g plain flour
- 3 cups milk, hot
- 100g Cheddar cheese, grated
- Salt and pepper, to taste
- 2 tablespoons breadcrumbs

Directions

- Preheat oven to 220°C.
- Steam or boil cauliflower for 7 minutes, or until tender. Drain and place in an ovenproof dish.
- Melt butter in a saucepan.
- Add flour; stirring to form a paste (roux).
- Gradually add milk, stirring until smooth.
- Simmer for 5 minutes, stirring constantly until mixture thickens.
- Remove from heat, then stir in grated cheese. Lightly season with salt and pepper.
- Pour mixture over cauliflower, then sprinkle with breadcrumbs and grated cheese.
- Bake for 20 minutes or until browned lightly.

Nutrition: This recipe will support your baby's liver and gut health. It is also a good source of protein, calcium and folate.

Mushroom Ratatouille

Ingredients

- 1 cup aubergine, diced
- 2 tablespoons olive oil
- 1 cup mushrooms, diced
- 1 small red onion, diced
- 1 clove garlic, minced
- 1 cup red pepper, diced
- 1 cup courgette, diced
- 400g can chopped tomatoes
- 1 beef stock cube
- 1 teaspoon sugar
- Salt and pepper, optional

Directions

- Place the aubergine in a colander, sprinkle with salt; stand for 10 minutes then rinse off salt and pat them dry. (Aubergines sometimes contain bitter juices, which can be released and removed by salting.)

- Heat 1 tablespoon of the olive oil in a saucepan over medium heat. Add the mushrooms and sauté until brown. Set aside.

- In the same pan, heat 1 tablespoon of olive oil. Add the onion, garlic and peppers; sauté, stirring for about 5 minutes or until the onion is soft.

- Add aubergine and courgette; cook while stirring for about 5 minutes or until aubergine is browned slightly.

- Return the mushroom to the saucepan. Add stock cube and simmer for 5 minutes.

- Add chopped tomatoes and sugar. If using, season with salt and black pepper to taste. Simmer, covered for about 20 minutes or until the vegetables are tender.

Nutrition: This immunity-boosting recipe is a great source of vitamin C, vitamin A and folate as well as dietary fibre and trace minerals.

Aubergine (Garden Egg) Sauce

Ingredients

- 1 medium aubergine, (you can use garden egg as a substitute)
- 3 tablespoons palm oil
- ½ red onion, finely diced
- 2 smoked mackerel fillets, shredded
- ½ tablespoon locust beans (iru)
- 1 beef stock cube
- ½ tablespoon ground crayfish
- 3 medium tomatoes
- 3 pointy sweet peppers (tatashe)
- Scotch bonnet pepper, to taste (optional)
- 1 garlic clove
- ½ teaspoon curry powder
- ½ teaspoon dried thyme

Directions

- Blend tomatoes, garlic, tatashe, and scotch bonnet pepper (if you are using it) to a smooth consistency.
- Wash the aubergine, then peel and dice. Place in a blender and purée to desired consistency.
- Heat palm oil in a medium saucepan. Sauté onion for 5 minutes, or until translucent.
- Add the tomato mixture, iru and beef stock cube. Simmer on medium-low heat for 15 minutes.
- Pour in puréed aubergine, mackerel and crayfish. Let simmer for 25-30 minutes, or until aubergine is tender.
- Serve with boiled yam, boiled potato, or boiled plantain.

Nutrition: Eggplant, also known as aubergine, garden egg, guinea squash, melongene, and brinja, is a very good source of dietary fibre, vitamin B1, and copper. It is a good source of manganese, vitamin B6, niacin, potassium, folate, and vitamin K. Eggplant also contains phytonutrients such as nasunin and chlorogenic acid.

Homemade Chicken Nuggets

Ingredients

- 1 chicken breast
- 1 cup plain flour
- 1 teaspoon Aromat seasoning
- ¼ teaspoon garlic powder
- ¼ teaspoon onion powder
- 1 egg
- 2 tablespoon milk
- 1 cup panko (a Japanese-style breadcrumb)
- ¼ teaspoon pepper
- ¼ teaspoon salt
- Vegetable oil, for frying

Directions

- Place the chicken breast in a sealable bag. Pound the chicken to its desired thickness, about ¼ inch. Dice into bite-size pieces and set aside.

- In a small bowl, combine the flour, Aromat, garlic powder and onion powder. Stir well to combine and transfer to a sealable bag.

- Place the chicken pieces in the bag with the flour and toss well to coat.

- Slightly beat the egg and 2 tablespoons of milk in a bowl, set aside.

- Place breadcrumbs onto a plate, season with salt and pepper.

- Dip each piece of chicken into the beaten egg and finally into the panko crumbs to coat evenly. Set aside on a clean plate.

- Heat vegetable oil in a medium frying pan over a medium-high heat. Working in batches, add the chicken pieces and brown each side until the chicken is cooked, usually about 8–10 minutes. Transfer the nuggets to a paper towel-lined plate to absorb excess oil.

- Serve with chips and steamed vegetables.

Nutrition: This meal is high in protein and a good source of B vitamins which help with energy production as well as vitamin D and vitamin A. Shop-bought chicken nuggets are often made with very poor quality chicken, so by making your own with diced chicken breast you can ensure that your baby gets the quality that he deserves.

Chicken Noodle Soup

Ingredients:

- 1 tablespoon vegetable oil
- 1 spring onion, chopped
- 1 garlic clove, minced
- 5 cups low salt chicken stock
- 1 medium carrot, cut diagonally into ½-inch thick slices
- 1 celery stalk, finely chopped
- 2 tablespoons sweetcorn
- 2 mushrooms, finely sliced
- 135g chicken breast
- 60g rice noodles
- ½ tablespoon soy sauce

Directions

- Place a pan over medium heat and coat with vegetable oil. Add onion, garlic, carrots, celery, sweetcorn and mushrooms. Stir for about 10 minutes, until the vegetables are softened but not browned. Remove vegetables and set aside.

- Pour in stock and add chicken. Bring to a boil, then reduce heat. Partly cover and simmer for 20 minutes, until chicken is tender. Carefully remove chicken to a cutting board. When cool enough to handle, discard the skin and bones; hand-shred the meat.

- Return chicken to the stock with the noodles, vegetables, and soy sauce. Simmer 5–6 minutes, until noodles are very tender.

Nutrition: Homemade chicken soup is often mentioned for its medicinal properties. It provides many of the key nutrients our immune systems need to function at their best, so cooking this recipe for your baby may help to ward off coughs and colds.

Spicy Turkey and Mushroom Bolognese

Ingredients

- 2 tablespoons olive oil
- 2 rashers of smoked streaky bacon, finely diced
- 1 garlic clove, minced
- 1 medium carrot, peeled and finely diced
- ½ cup button mushrooms, finely diced
- 1 small yellow onion, diced
- ½ celery stalk, trimmed and finely chopped
- 250g minced turkey
- 1 tin (400g) chopped tomatoes
- 1 teaspoon tomato paste
- 1 small chilli, finely chopped
- ¼ teaspoon mixed dried herbs
- ½ cup whole milk
- 1 beef stock cube
- Salt and black pepper, to taste
- Parmesan cheese for serving
- Your choice of pasta

Directions

- Heat olive oil in a saucepan over a medium-high heat; gently fry your bacon until golden. Reduce heat to medium then add the garlic and onions and cook, stirring constantly, until the onions are translucent, about 3 minutes. Add the carrot, mushrooms and celery and sauté until the vegetables are tender, about 5 minutes.

- Add the minced turkey to the pan, increase the heat to medium, cook until turkey is browned, stirring to crumble.

- Add the tinned tomatoes, tomato paste, chilli, herbs, stock cube and milk. Season with salt and pepper to taste.

- Reduce the heat to low-medium, put the lid on and cook the sauce, stirring occasionally, for 45–60 minutes. While sauce cooks, cook pasta according to package directions.

- When ready to serve, plate the pasta, top with the turkey Bolognese and sprinkle with Parmesan cheese. Serve immediately.

Nutrition: Not only is turkey a good lean protein source but it provides tryptophan, which helps to regulate our mood and sleep patterns. Mushrooms provide good quantities of selenium, vitamin D and iron amongst other nutrients and should if possible become a staple of your baby's diet.

Fruity Chicken Curry

Ingredients

- 1 tablespoon butter
- 300g chicken breast fillet, diced
- ½ small onion, finely chopped
- ½ cup carrot, peeled and diced
- 1 garlic clove, minced
- 1 tablespoon curry powder
- ½ cup sweet apple, cored and finely diced
- 2 cups chicken stock
- salt and pepper, to taste (optional)
- ½ cup coconut milk
- ¼ cup raisins
- ¼ cup dried apricots, finely chopped

Directions

- Melt butter in a saucepan over medium heat. Add chicken and brown on all sides for approximately 5 minutes. Set aside.

- Add onion, carrot, apricot and garlic to the same pan and sauté for 5 minutes. Stir in curry powder.

- Return chicken to pan; add apple and stock. Season with salt and black pepper, if using. Cover and simmer for 5 minutes. Add coconut milk and raisins. Bring to a boil and simmer, covered, for another 15 minutes, then cook uncovered for 10 minutes, or until sauce thickens.

Nutrition: This recipe is rich in phosphorus, an essential mineral that supports your baby's teeth and bones, as well as kidney, liver, and central nervous system function.

Nutrition: Chicken thighs are much higher in iron and other nutrients than chicken breasts, plus they taste better. The ginger in this recipe stimulates digestion and the onion provides pre-biotics, which feed the beneficial bacteria in your baby's gut.

Nigerian Chicken Stew

Ingredients

- 2 tablespoons vegetable oil
- 1 small onion, finely sliced
- 500g bone-in chicken thighs
- 1 teaspoon curry powder
- 1 teaspoon dried thyme
- ¼ teaspoon ground nutmeg
- 1 teaspoon Aromat seasoning
- 1 beef stock cube
- 3 tomatoes
- 2 large pointy sweet peppers
- 1 garlic clove
- 1 bay leaf
- 1 teaspoon ginger
- ¼ scotch bonnet pepper (optional)
- Salt, to taste (optional)

Directions

- Heat 1 tablespoon of oil over medium heat. Sauté ½ of the onions for 5 minutes or until tender. Place the chicken in a medium saucepan and brown on all sides for about 5 minutes. Add curry, thyme, nutmeg, Aromat seasoning and stock cube; simmer on a low heat for another 2 minutes.

- Pour in water to just cover the chicken. Bring to a boil and simmer on medium-low heat for 30 minutes.

- Meanwhile place the tomatoes, pointy peppers, garlic, ginger and scotch bonnet (if using) in a blender. Purée till smooth.

- Pour the puréed tomato mixture into a saucepan and simmer on a medium-low heat for 20 minutes. Add the remaining oil and onions and simmer on low heat for a further 15 minutes or until the tomato mixture thickens.

- For younger children you can dice the chicken and discard the bones. For older kids, you don't have to. Add the chicken and bay leaf to the tomato mixture and pour in stock. Season with salt if needed. Simmer on low heat for another 15–20 minutes.

Kids' Sweet and Sour Chicken

Ingredients

- 160g boneless, skinless chicken breasts
- Salt and pepper, to taste
- 2 tablespoons cornflour
- 2 tablespoons vegetable oil, for frying
- 2 eggs
- 1/3 cup green pepper, diced
- 1/3cup red pepper, diced
- 1 garlic clove, minced
- 1 teaspoon fresh grated ginger
- ½ cup pineapple chunks
- 1 stalk spring onion, finely chopped

Sweet and sour sauce

- 1 tablespoon brown sugar
- 2 tablespoons rice wine vinegar
- 2 tablespoons ketchup
- 1 teaspoon soy sauce
- ¼ teaspoon Tabasco sauce
- ½ teaspoon Worcestershire sauce
- ½ cup pineapple juice (optional)
- ¼ cup chicken stock (optional)

Nutrition: This recipe provides protein and fibre as well as vitamin C, vitamin B6 and vitamin B12. The pineapple provides digestive enzymes and a sweetness, without making the dish overly sweet. If you use a homemade chicken stock, then the mineral content of this dish will be much higher.

Directions

- Preheat oven to 160°C. Lightly oil a medium-sized baking dish or coat with non-stick spray.

- Mix the sweet and sour sauce ingredients in a small bowl and set aside.

- Cut the chicken breast meat into bite-size cubes and marinate with salt and pepper for 10 minutes. Place the cornflour into a sealable bag, add chicken and toss to coat.

- Heat the vegetable oil in a large saucepan. In a shallow dish, whisk together the eggs. Working one at a time, dip the cornflour-covered chicken pieces into the beaten egg, coating both sides.

- Cook the chicken until golden brown, about 1–2 minutes. Transfer the chicken out on a plate lined with paper towels to soak up the excess oil.

- In the same pan, sauté the green pepper, red pepper, garlic, ginger, pineapple and spring onion for 2 minutes.

- Add the chicken to the baking dish. Mix in the sautéed vegetables and pour the sweet and sour sauce over the sautéed chicken and vegetables, tossing to coat. Place into oven and bake for 45–60 minutes, until the sauce has thickened, turning over occasionally to evenly coat the chicken.

- Serve with basmati rice.

Nutrition: By making your own chicken wings using this recipe, you get all the delicious taste but without the additives. Baking your chicken wings is much healthier than frying them.

Micah's Favourite Chicken Wings

Ingredients

- 550g chicken wings

For the marinade

- 1 cup tomato ketchup
- ½ tablespoon Worcestershire sauce
- 2½ tablespoons soy sauce
- ½ teaspoon Tabasco sauce (optional)
- 1 teaspoon brown sugar
- 1 small onion, finely diced
- 1 beef stock cube, crushed
- 1 teaspoon Aromat seasoning
- 1 teaspoon curry powder
- 1 teaspoon mixed herbs
- 1 garlic clove, minced
- ½ tablespoon vegetable oil

Directions

- Rinse chicken wings and pat dry with paper towels.
- Mix together all marinade ingredients and pour over chicken. Marinate in refrigerator for at least 2 hours, or overnight if possible.
- Preheat oven to 180°C.
- Place wings in a single layer on a lightly-greased baking tray. Top with a couple of spoonfuls of marinade and place in oven. Cook for 20–25 minutes, turning occasionally and basting with marinade and juices until thoroughly sticky and golden.
- Serve with homemade potato wedges or fries and steamed vegetables.

Chicken Egusi Soup

Ingredients

- 600g bone-in chicken pieces
- 1 small onion, finely diced
- 1 beef stock cube
- 1 teaspoon Aromat seasoning
- 1 pointy sweet pepper
- scotch bonnet pepper (optional)
- 1 tablespoon ground crayfish
- ½ cup cooked, shredded stockfish
- 2 tablespoons palm oil
- 1 ½ cups ground egusi (dried melon seeds)
- Handful of finely chopped spinach or leafy vegetable of your choice

Directions

- In a medium saucepan, add enough water to cover chicken. Add 1 stock cube, Aromat seasoning, and half of the onion, then bring to a boil and simmer for 15 minutes.

- Add pointy pepper, scotch bonnet pepper, and ¼ cup of water to a blender; purée to a smooth consistency. Transfer to the saucepan with chicken. Season with salt to taste. Add stockfish, bring to a boil, and then simmer for another 15 minutes.

- Meanwhile, heat palm oil in a separate saucepan. Sauté remaining onions for 5 minutes. Add ground crayfish and fry for a further 3 minutes. Add egusi and remaining stock cube (if you want a thicker soup, you can add more). Give it a good stir and then simmer, covered, for 10 minutes.

- Transfer egusi to the chicken mixture and add in chopped spinach. Simmer uncovered for an additional 15 minutes.

Nutrition: Egusi is rich in protein, B vitamins, minerals, and fat. Stockfish is extremely nutritious and truly healthy. It is also rich in essential ingredients such as vitamin B12, niacin, and thiamine, which help to maintain your baby's nerves and ensure normal growth. It also provides phosphorous, which is needed for the effective utilisation of calories, iodine to help keep your little one's thyroid gland healthy and ensure normal metabolism, and plenty of calcium for strong bones and teeth.

Sweet Potato Shepherd's Pie

Kids will love the twist on this traditional dish: sweet potato topping! It not only adds a fantastic colour but a great taste, too.

Ingredients

- 2 tablespoons olive oil
- 250g quality minced beef
- ¼ cup finely chopped onions
- 1 medium carrot, finely chopped
- ¼ cup finely diced celery stalk
- 1 garlic clove, minced
- 1 tablespoon cornflour
- 1 tablespoon tomato purée
- 1¼ cups beef stock
- 1 teaspoon Worcestershire sauce
- 1 cup frozen peas
- Salt and pepper, to taste

Sweet Potato Topping:

- 600g sweet potatoes, peeled and finely diced
- 3 tablespoons melted butter
- 3 tablespoons warm milk

Directions

- Heat 1 tablespoon of olive oil in a medium saucepan; add minced beef, and season lightly with salt and pepper. Break up meat until it is browned, then remove beef and juices from the pan and set aside.

- In the same pan, pour in the remaining olive oil. Add onions, carrots, celery, and garlic. Sauté for 5 to 7 minutes, or until onions are translucent.

- Return the browned beef to the saucepan and mix contents together. Add cornflour and cook for 2 minutes. Add tomato paste and cook for another minute.

- Add stock and Worcestershire sauce. Bring to a boil, then reduce heat and simmer for 15 minutes, or until thickened slightly. Add in frozen peas and cook for an additional 5 minutes. Season to taste with salt and pepper.

- While the meat is cooking, heat oven to 180°C and then place potatoes and a pinch of salt into a pot of cold water, cover, and bring to a boil. Remove cover and boil for another 15 minutes, until fork tender. Drain, then mash with butter to desired consistency.

- Divide the mince mixture between 4 ramekins, then top with mashed potatoes and ruffle with a fork.

- If preparing your child's meal in advance, the shepherd's pie can now be frozen for up to 4 weeks.

- Bake for 35 minutes, or until the topping starts to brown.

- Let stand 15 minutes before serving.

Nutrition: This recipe provides lots of good quality protein, which your baby needs during this period of rapid growth. The beef is a very good source of iron and zinc (amongst other nutrients) — two minerals which children often don't get enough of in their daily diet.

Beef Stroganoff

Ingredients

- 2 beef sirloin steaks, cut in strips

- Black pepper and salt, to taste

- 1 tablespoon butter

- 1 tablespoon olive oil

- 1 shallot, finely chopped

- 7 button mushrooms, finely diced

- 1 teaspoon tomato purée

- 1 teaspoon brown sugar

- 1 tablespoon cornflour

- 1 cup beef stock

- 2 tablespoons crème fraiche

Directions

- Season the beef with black pepper and salt.

- In a non-stick pan, heat half of the butter and half of the oil. Increase to a medium-high heat and place the beef in the pan, cooking both sides, at least 4 minutes on each side. When both sides are browned, transfer the beef to a plate and set aside.

- In the same pan, heat the remaining butter and oil, add the shallots and sauté until translucent, about 5 minutes. Add the mushrooms and fry gently for 5 minutes.

- Stir in the tomato purée, sugar and cornflour, then gradually stir in the stock.

- Add the beef, bring to a boil and simmer on low heat until the sauce thickens.

- Stir in the crème fraiche and serve with fluffy rice or pasta.

Nutrition: The recipe provides a good balance of protein, carbohydrate and fat and if you can use grass-fed beef, it is also a source of omega-3 fats.

Beef and Broccoli Chow Mein

This recipe involves velveting the beef, which results in meat that is silky soft and lusciously tender.

Ingredients

- 150g sirloin steak (for younger toddlers you can use minced beef instead)
- Vegetable oil
- ½ small yellow onion
- 1 garlic clove, minced
- 1 teaspoon fresh ginger, minced
- 1 small carrot, julienned
- 1 teaspoon cornflour
- ¼ cup beef stock
- 120g Chinese egg noodles
- 1 cup broccoli florets
- 1 tablespoon soy sauce
- 1 tablespoon oyster sauce
- ½ tablespoon rice vinegar
- ½ teaspoon brown sugar
- Salt and pepper, to taste

Velveting

- 1 egg white
- 1 tablespoon Chinese rice wine vinegar/ Chinese rice vinegar
- 1 tablespoon cornflour
- Pinch of salt

Directions

- Dry the beef well, using kitchen towels, and slice thinly.

- In a bowl, combine the egg white, salt, Chinese rice wine and cornflour. Whisk together until the cornflour dissolves and the mixture is smooth and frothy. Add the beef and marinate in the refrigerator for one hour. Using a colander, drain the beef.

- Fill a medium saucepan with water and add one teaspoon of oil. Bring to a boil. Reduce heat to medium low and immediately add beef, stirring to disperse. Bring water back to a gentle simmer and, once it's barely bubbling, continue to cook the beef for about 1 minute, stirring occasionally. With a slotted spoon, remove the beef from the pot, drain well and set aside.

- Cook the noodles according to the package instructions. Rinse under cold water, drain and set aside.

- In a medium bowl, mix the sugar, oyster sauce, rice vinegar and soy sauce together. Mix the beef stock and the cornflour together then stir in the thickened beef stock. Set aside.

- Heat 1 tablespoon of oil in a pan over a high heat. Add the beef and stir fry until just browned. Transfer the meat and any juices to a plate.

- Heat 1 tablespoon of oil in the same pan over a high heat. Add the onion, ginger and garlic. Sauté for 3 minutes or until the onion has softened. Add the carrot and cook, stirring for 5 minutes or until the carrot starts to soften.

- Add the broccoli, beef and the soy/stock mixture. Cook, stirring occasionally, for 5 minutes or until the broccoli is tender. Add noodles and toss everything together until combined and heated through – about 2 minutes. Serve hot.

Nutrition: This meal is substantial, wholesome and satisfying. Beef is an excellent source of iron, B vitamins and many essential minerals and it provides complete protein. The vegetables provide fibre, vitamins and phytonutrients and the egg noodles are a great addition to your baby's carbohydrate rotation.

Nutrition: In general, it's a good idea to eat from all parts of an animal because each part provides different nutritional value. Choosing an assortment of vegetables to use in your oxtail curry will help increase the overall nutritional content of your oxtail dish.

Yummy Oxtail Curry

Ingredients

- 650g oxtail, trimmed of fat

- 1 small onion, finely diced

- 1 garlic clove, minced

- 1 tablespoon coconut oil

- 1 tablespoon curry powder

- 1 cup coconut milk

- 2½ cups water

- 2 beef stock cubes

- 1 sprig fresh thyme

- Pinch of nutmeg

- 1 small scotch bonnet (pepper), optional

- salt to taste, optional

Marinade

- ½ tablespoon curry powder

- ¼ cup ketchup

- 1 tomato, finely diced

- 1 carrot, finely diced

- 1 celery stalk, trimmed and diced

Directions

- In a bowl, mix together the oxtail, ketchup, tomato, celery and curry powder. Marinade for at least 1 hour.

- Heat the coconut oil in a saucepan, sauté the garlic and onion for 5 minutes. Add the curry powder and stir in. Add the marinated oxtail pieces with the tomatoes, carrots and celery and fry until brown all over.

- Add the coconut milk, water, nutmeg, beef stock cubes and salt, if using. Give it a good stir and top with fresh thyme and scotch bonnet.

- Bring to a boil, then turn down the heat to a gentle simmer. Cover and cook for 3½–4 hours, until the oxtail is really tender and falling off the bone.

- Serve with couscous and vegetables.

Nutrition: This wonderfully balanced dish provides good quality protein, essential fats and complex carbohydrate in the ideal proportions. Prawns are a good source of cholesterol (which babies need) and heart-healthy omega-3 fats. This recipe also provides selenium, magnesium and zinc, all of which are essential for your baby's hormone production. The garlic and onions contain gut friendly pre-biotics and the peas provide B vitamins for energy.

Surf and Turf Fried Rice

Ingredients

- 2 cups cooked rice
- 1 egg
- 1 teaspoon sesame oil
- 2 tablespoons vegetable oil
- 1 garlic clove, minced
- 1 teaspoon Aromat seasoning
- ½ cup frozen peas
- 1 spring onion, finely chopped
- 2 teaspoons soy sauce
- ¾ cup small, cooked prawns
- 1 cup grilled or cooked chicken breast, finely shredded

Directions

- Boil the rice according to packaging instructions, set aside.
- Beat the egg together with the sesame oil, set aside.
- Heat oil in a large frying pan or wok. Add the garlic, rice and Aromat seasoning, stir fry for 3 minutes, push to the corner of the pan. Pour the egg in the opposite corner of the pan, then scramble, stirring.
- Once set, stir in the spring onions, peas, chicken, prawns and soy sauce. Cook for a further 5 minutes until the peas are tender.

Nutrition: Sardines are an excellent source of DHA, which your baby needs for her brain, heart and eye development. This recipe provides both calcium and magnesium, which your baby needs to build strong bones and it is also a great introduction to spices.

Sardine Fusilli

Ingredients

- 2½ cups fusilli pasta
- 2 tomatoes
- 1 pointy pepper
- 1 teaspoon fresh ginger
- 1 garlic clove
- 1 small chilli (optional)
- 1 tablespoon vegetable oil
- ½ onion, finely diced
- 1 carrot, peeled and diced
- ½ teaspoon curry powder
- ½ teaspoon dried thyme
- Beef stock cube
- 1 mackerel fillet
- 95g boneless sardine in sunflower oil, reserve the oil
- ¼ cup peas

Directions

- Cook the pasta according to packing instructions, set aside.

- Meanwhile, purée the tomatoes, pointy pepper, ginger, garlic and chilli (if using) to a smooth purée.

- Heat 2 tablespoons of the sardine oil and the vegetable oil in a saucepan, sauté onion for 3 minutes. Add carrots and sauté for another 2 minutes. Pour in your blended tomato mixture, curry, thyme and stock cube. Simmer on a medium-low heat, stirring occasionally for 15 minutes. Add the mackerel fillet, sardine and peas and cook for a further 15 minutes, breaking up the mackerel and sardine with a spoon.

- When the sauce thickens, pour in the cooked fusilli and toss to combine. Cook for a further 3 minutes.

Salmon Couscous

Ingredients

- 115g salmon fillet
- 3 tablespoons honey
- 1 tablespoon soy sauce
- 1 garlic clove, minced
- 1 teaspoon butter
- ¼ cup finely diced onion
- ½ cup crushed tomatoes
- pinch of curry
- pinch of nutmeg
- 2 cups chicken stock
- Handful of broccoli florets, or your child's favourite vegetable
- 1 ½ cups couscous

Directions

- Preheat oven to 200°C.

- Mix honey, soy sauce and garlic together in a bowl. Pour mixture over salmon fillet in a sealable bag, coating it. Marinate for at least 30 minutes, or preferably up to 2 hours.

- Bake the salmon for 12 minutes, turning over halfway.

- Meanwhile, melt butter in a saucepan. Add onions and sauté for 5 minutes. Add crushed tomatoes and simmer on low heat for 10 minutes.

- Add chicken stock, curry, nutmeg and one tablespoon of unused marinade to the saucepan. Add broccoli. Bring to a boil, then reduce heat to low and allow to simmer for 7 minutes.

- Remove from heat. Stir in couscous; cover and allow couscous to sit for 7 minutes, until fluffy and all the stock has been absorbed

- Flake salmon into the couscous and broccoli mixture and fluff couscous with a fork.

Nutrition: After your baby is a year old, he or she can enjoy honey, which is packed full of antioxidants, B vitamins and zinc. Salmon is a great source of omega-3 fats, especially if you can choose wild salmon in place of farmed. This recipe is also great for including a variety of vegetables.

Crayfish Tail Coconut Rice

Ingredients

- 2 cups basmati rice
- 200g cooked crayfish tails
- 1 cup coconut milk
- ½ cup tin chopped tomatoes
- 2 ½ cups chicken stock
- ½ cup green pepper, deseeded and finely diced
- ½ cup yellow pepper, deseeded and finely diced
- ½ cup red pepper, deseeded and finely diced
- ½ cup carrot, peeled and finely diced
- ½ cup sweetcorn
- ½ yellow onion, finely diced
- Scotch bonnet pepper, to taste (optional)
- ¼ teaspoon curry
- ¼ teaspoon dried thyme
- 2 tablespoons coconut oil
- 1 ½ tablespoon ground crayfish
- 1 beef stock cube

Directions

- Heat coconut oil in a saucepan. Add onions and sauté for 3 minutes. Add peppers, carrots, scotch bonnet (if using), ground crayfish, and beef stock cube. Simmer on low heat for 10 minutes. Add crayfish tail and sweetcorn, then simmer 5 additional minutes.

- Meanwhile, in another saucepan, add chopped tomatoes, chicken stock, and coconut milk. Cook for 5 minutes.

- Add rice and stir. Bring to a simmer, then cover with aluminum foil and the lid for another 15 minutes.

- Add the crayfish tails and vegetable mixture; let simmer for 10 more minutes, or until the rice has absorbed all the juices.

Nutrition: Crayfish is rich in minerals such as calcium, magnesium, iron, and potassium. It is also a fantastic source of cholesterol, which babies need for optimal brain development. Breast milk contains a lot of cholesterol, but as babies begin to take less milk they need to get more from their diets. Coconut is a good source of monounsaturated fats and lauric acid, which is found in high concentrations in breast milk but scarcely anywhere else in nature.

Nutrition: This recipe provides all the benefits of the marinara sauce (page 231) as well as good quality protein and B vitamins, which your baby needs for energy. If you can find grass-fed beef this is preferable to the conventionally-fed variety as it has a much higher omega-3 content.

Spaghetti and Meatballs

Ingredients

- 500g minced beef
- 1 medium yellow onion, finely diced
- ¼ cup Parmesan, grated, plus extra to serve if you like
- ½ cup breadcrumbs
- 1 egg, beaten
- ¼ teaspoon curry powder
- ½ teaspoon Aromat seasoning
- ½ teaspoon Italian herb seasoning
- Extra virgin olive oil
- Spaghetti, to serve

Marinara sauce, recipe on page 231

Directions

- In a medium bowl, combine the mince, onion, Parmesan, breadcrumbs, beaten egg, curry powder, Aromat and Italian herb seasoning. Squish the mixture with your hands to mix together really well. Roll a level tablespoon of mixture to form each meatball. You can make it bigger or smaller, depending on how your child likes it.

- Heat the olive oil in a medium saucepan and cook the meatballs, uncovered, until brown. Alternatively, heat the oven to 200°C, place the meatballs on a roasting tray and drizzle with a little oil and bake them for 20 minutes or until browned.

- Meanwhile make the marinara sauce. Then add meatballs to sauce and simmer on a very low heat for 2 minutes. Set aside, covered.

- Cook the spaghetti according to packaging instructions.

- Serve the spaghetti topped with the meatballs and a sprinkle of grated Parmesan.

Kid-friendly Lasagne Bolognese

Ingredients

- 2 tablespoons olive oil
- 1 garlic clove, minced
- 1 small yellow onion, finely diced
- 1 small carrot, peeled and finely diced
- 1 small stalk celery, trimmed and finely diced
- 2 slices pancetta, chopped finely
- 1 cup milk
- 400g tin chopped tomatoes
- 1 beef stock cube
- 1 cup beef stock
- ¼ teaspoon dried mixed Italian herbs
- 250g beef mince

Béchamel Sauce

- 30g butter
- 30g plain flour
- 1 ½ cups whole milk
- Pinch of nutmeg

Lasagne

- 6–8 egg lasagne sheets
- 50g grated Parmesan
- Freshly ground black pepper

Directions

- Heat olive oil in a large saucepan. Cook celery, onions, carrot, garlic, and pancetta, stirring until vegetables soften.

- Add minced beef, stirring until browned. Use a wooden spoon to break lumps of mince.

- Add milk, tomatoes, dried herbs, and stock cube.

- Bring to a boil and simmer, uncovered, for 1½ hours, or until meat is tender and sauce has thickened. Season as needed.

- To make the béchamel sauce, melt butter in a medium saucepan. Add flour and cook for 2 minutes, stirring until the mixture forms a smooth paste. Gradually add milk, stirring constantly to avoid lumps. When all the milk is in, bring to a gentle simmer, stirring until sauce boils and thickens. Remove from heat, then add Parmesan and season with nutmeg, salt, and pepper to taste.

- Meanwhile, preheat oven to 200°C and grease a baking dish.

- For the lasagne, blanch the pasta in salted boiling water for 3 minutes.

- Spread a spoonful of the Bolognese sauce over the base of the dish. Cover with single layer of sheets of lasagne. Spoon on more Bolognese sauce, a small amount of white sauce, and a sprinkle of grated Parmesan.

- Repeat the layering process, ending with a final layer of pasta sheet, then top with sprinkled Parmesan.

- Bake for 30 minutes, or until lightly browned. Let stand 10 minutes before serving.

Nutrition: This classic lasagne dish is well-balanced in terms of quality protein, complex carbohydrates and healthy fats.

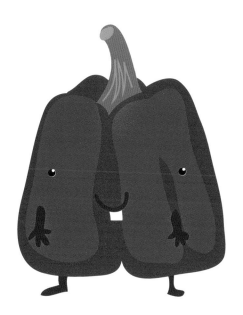

Pasta with Hidden Vegetable Sauce

Kids will always eat pasta with tomato sauce but they won't always eat their vegetables so it can help to magically, mysteriously hide them in the sauce. This is the sort of sauce that you may end up making on a regular basis, so this recipe prepares a large quantity.

Ingredients

- 1 tablespoon olive oil
- 1 small onion, chopped
- 1 celery stick chopped
- 1 carrot, peeled and chopped
- ½ leek, chopped (white and light green parts only)
- 2 x 400g tin chopped tomatoes
- 1 garlic clove, crushed
- 1 red pepper, chopped
- ¼ teaspoon curry powder
- ¼ teaspoon mixed dried herbs
- 1 beef stock cube
- Salt and pepper to taste (optional)
- Pinch of dried mixed herbs

Directions

- Heat the olive oil in a large saucepan, gently sauté all the vegetables for 5 minutes. Add the stock cube, curry and mixed dried herbs and sauté for a further 5 minutes.

- Add the tomatoes, have a taste and season with a little salt or pepper if needed.

- Stir to combine, then cover and simmer for about 30–45 minutes until vegetables are very tender.

- Transfer the mixture to a blender and blitz it until smooth.

- Serve with your kid's favourite pasta.

Nutrition: This recipe is a good source of vitamin K, which your baby needs for proper blood clotting. It also provides vitamin B6, iron, folate, and vitamin C, all of which are required for maintaining strong blood and a healthy immune system. The vegetables in this dish provide vitamin A, which is good for your baby's eyesight, and omega-3 fatty acids.

Marinara Sauce

This pasta sauce recipe can be used as a base for so many dishes.

Ingredients

- 2 tablespoons olive oil
- 1 small yellow onion, diced finely
- 2 cloves garlic, minced
- 2 x 400g tin chopped tomatoes
- 1 teaspoon caster sugar
- 1 tablespoon chopped fresh flat-leaf parsley
- Salt, to taste
- Pepper, to taste

Directions

- Heat the olive oil over a medium heat in a saucepan, sauté the onion and garlic for 5 minutes until the onion softens.
- Stir in the tomatoes, sugar, parsley, season with salt and pepper. Bring to a boil and simmer on a low heat for 15 minutes or until the sauce thickens.

Nutrition: This recipe is a good source of lycopene, a powerful antioxidant as well as vitamins C and A and zinc. Parsley is one of the best known plant sources of vitamin K, which your baby needs for proper blood clotting.

Nutrition: This recipe has anti-inflammatory, antimicrobial and antiviral properties so it is useful for keeping colds at bay. It also provides complex carbohydrates, vitamins C, A, D, K and the whole B complex. The rainbow variety of vegetables provides health promoting phytonutrients and lots of fibre to keep your baby's digestive system working at its best.

Penne with Vegetables

Ingredients

- 1 tablespoon olive oil
- ½ small onion, peeled and diced
- 1 garlic clove, minced
- ½ cup diced red pepper
- ½ cup diced yellow pepper
- ½ cup diced courgette
- ½ cup diced mushrooms
- ½ teaspoon dried Italian herb mix
- 1 beef stock cube
- 2 medium tomatoes, diced
- Black pepper, to taste
- 1½ cups penne pasta

Directions

- Heat the olive oil in a medium saucepan. Sauté the onion and garlic until onion is translucent.
- Add the red pepper, yellow pepper, courgette, mushrooms and dried herbs.
- Sauté for a further 5 minutes.
- Add ½ cup of water, tomatoes, stock cube and black pepper, to taste. Bring to a boil and simmer for 20 minutes until the vegetables are tender.
- Meanwhile cook the penne according to packaging instructions.
- Mix your cooked pasta with your vegetable mixture and let it simmer for 3 minutes.

Toddlers

	Breakfast (7am)	Mid-morning (9.30am)	Lunch (12.00pm/12.30pm)	
Monday	Pancakes, finely chopped fruit yoghurt	Drink of water plus finely diced vegetables, fruits or finger foods	Surf and Turf Fried Rice, quartered fresh apple, water	
Tuesday	Pear Semolina, Breakfast Smoothie	Drink of water plus finely diced vegetables, fruits or finger foods	Spicy Turkey and Mushroom Bolognese kiwi fruit slices, water	
Wednesday	Boiled egg with lightly buttered toast fingers, finely chopped fruit	Drink of water plus finely diced vegetables, fruits or finger foods	Micah's Favourite Chicken Wings with fries and vegetables, yoghurt, water	
Thursday	Weetabix, yoghurt with fruits, breastfeed or formula milk	Drink of water plus finely diced vegetables, fruits or finger foods	Sweet Potato Shepherds Pie, finely diced strawberries, water	
Friday	Fruitilicious Oatmeal	Drink of water plus finely diced vegetables, fruits or finger foods	Spicy Turkey and Mushroom Bolognese kiwi fruit slices, water	
Saturday	Plantain Frittata, finely chopped fruit	Drink of water plus finely diced vegetables, fruits or finger foods	Potato Pottage, quartered fresh pear, water	
Sunday	Weetabix, sliced fresh fruit with yoghurt dip	Drink of water plus finely diced vegetables, fruits or finger foods	Fruity Chicken Curry with couscous, diced papaya, water	

Mid-afternoon (2.30pm)	Tea (5.30pm)	Bedtime (7.00pm)
Drink of water plus finely diced vegetables, fruits or finger foods	Potato Pottage, quartered fresh pear, water	Breastfeed or formula milk
Drink of water plus finely diced vegetables, fruits or finger foods	Fruity Chicken Curry with couscous, diced papaya, water	Breastfeed or formula milk
Drink of water plus finely diced vegetables, fruits or finger foods	Aubergine Sauce with fried plantain, water	Breastfeed or formula milk
Drink of water plus finely diced vegetables, fruits or finger foods	Surf and Turf Fried Rice, quartered fresh apple, water	Breastfeed or formula milk
Drink of water plus finely diced vegetables, fruits or finger foods	Okra Soup with Amala, water	Breastfeed or formula milk
Drink of water plus finely diced vegetables, fruits or finger foods	Aubergine Sauce with fried plantain, water	Breastfeed or formula milk
Drink of water plus finely diced vegetables, fruits or finger foods	Selection of mini sandwiches, yoghurt, water	Breastfeed or formula milk

Nutrition: This is such a clever way to get more vegetables into babies and young children. Courgette is a great source of vitamin C, potassium and dietary fibre and is generally much more nutrient-dense than potato. Serve with guacamole or hummus for added protein and essential fats.

Finger Foods

Cheese cubes, naturally soft fruits and vegetables such as banana coins, mango squares, diced watermelon, diced kiwi fruit, avocado slices, cucumber sticks, pepper strips, courgette sticks, shredded coconut.

Lightly steamed vegetables such as broccoli and cauliflower florets, carrot sticks, green peas and green beans.

Some more ideas:

Courgette Fries

Ingredients

- 1 courgette, peeled and quartered lengthwise

- ½ cup panko

- ¼ cup finely grated Parmesan

- ½ cup plain flour

- Pinch of garlic powder

- 1 teaspoon Italian dried herbs

- 1 egg

- 1 tablespoon milk

- Salt and pepper to taste, optional

Directions

- Preheat oven to 220°C. Line a baking tray with greased parchment paper or aluminium foil.

- Beat eggs in a small bowl and add milk.

- Combine the panko, Parmesan, Italian herbs, garlic and salt and pepper, if using. Mix thoroughly.

- Place the plain flour in a sealable bag, add the courgette and toss to coat.

- Working one at a time, dip the flour-covered courgette fries into the egg mixture, coating both sides. Then press each courgette stick into the breadcrumbs to coat.

- Bake in the preheated oven until the fries are golden and crispy – about 20 minutes.

- Serve immediately with your child's favourite dip.

Nutrition: Plantain provides complex carbohydrates, which fuel your baby's muscles, brain and other cells and tissues. Plantain chips offer more vitamin A and vitamin C compared to potato chips, both of which help keep your baby's skin healthy and benefit their immune system to keep them free of infection. Plantain chips also have a higher protein content than potato chips.

Homemade Sweet Plantain Chips

My son loves snacking on plantain chips, but most plantain chips you find in supermarkets are too salty or too sweet. So I decided to start making homemade plantain chips. They are healthier, cheaper and taste so much better. You can also mix and match spices for your plantain chips.

Ingredients

- 1 large ripe plantain
- Pinch of nutmeg
- Pinch of caster sugar
- Vegetable oil for frying

Directions

- Peel and thinly slice the plantain using a mandolin slicer set on one of the thinnest settings.

- In a medium bowl toss the plantain slices with nutmeg and sugar, mixing well to ensure the plantain is thoroughly coated.

- Heat the oil and fry the plantain in batches until golden brown and crispy.

Nutrition: Sweet potato brownies must be one of the healthiest cakes you could possibly make for your baby. They are packed with antioxidants, vitamin C, and manganese, which help to oxygenate the blood. The sweet potato is a great source of fibre and, as they don't contain any sugar, the whole family can enjoy this treat regularly.

Sweet Potato Brownie

Ingredients

- 2 sweet potatoes, peeled and diced
- 1 egg
- 100g plain flour
- ¼ cup crystallised coconut nectar
- ¼ teaspoon vanilla extract
- 5 tablespoons cocoa powder
- ¼ teaspoon baking powder
- Handful of chocolate chips (optional)
- 2 tablespoons butter, melted

Directions

- Preheat oven to 180°C.
- Boil or steam the sweet potatoes until tender, then purée in a food processor or blender.
- In a bowl combine mashed potatoes, butter, eggs, and coconut nectar. Mix well.
- In another bowl, whisk together baking powder, flour, and cocoa powder. Add the dry ingredient mixture to the sweet potato mixture and stir until just combined. Stir in chocolate chips, if you are using them.
- Once combined, pour mixture into a baking tray lined with greased baking paper.
- Bake for 25–35 minutes, or until a fork is dry after piercing the brownie. Remove tray and cool for 10 minutes. Remove brownies from tray and cut into squares.

Cauliflower Popcorn

Ingredients

- 1 head of cauliflower, cut into small florets
- 3 tablespoons coconut oil
- 3 tablespoons maple syrup

Directions

- Preheat oven to 220°C.
- In a large bowl combine the cauliflower, oil and maple syrup. Transfer to a baking sheet and spread in a single layer.
- Roast in the oven stirring every 10 minutes until golden brown and tender – about 30 minutes.

Nutrition: Cauliflower is a good source of choline, a B vitamin known for its role in brain development. Choline may boost your baby's cognitive function, and improve learning and memory. The coconut oil provides saturated fats, which your baby needs plenty of during this period of rapid growth and maple syrup is my preferred sweetener for children because of its high antioxidant content.

Beetroot Chips

Ingredients

- 2 medium beets, rinsed and scrubbed
- 1 tablespoon olive oil

Directions

- Preheat oven to 190°C.
- Thinly slice the beets with a mandolin or sharp knife. Try to make slices consistently thick to ensure even baking and crispiness.
- In a large bowl, toss the beet slices with olive oil to coat evenly, then arrange in a single layer on 2 baking sheets. Bake for 15 minutes until brown and crispy.

Nutrition: Beetroot is amazing for strengthening the blood as it provides a good dose of folate, manganese, copper and potassium. Don't be surprised if your baby's urine has a slight red tinge after eating lots of these chips; it's perfectly normal and healthy.

Green Pea Purée

Ingredients

- 2 cups green peas
- 1 garlic clove, minced
- 1 tablespoon butter
- 1 teaspoon honey
- 3 tablespoons natural yoghurt

Directions

- Melt the butter in a saucepan.
- Sauté the garlic and green peas for 5 minutes.
- Add the yoghurt and blend to a smooth consistency.
- Mix in honey.

Nutrition: This purée provides flavinoids, carotenoids and polyphenols, which will help to keep your baby's immune system strong. It is also antimicrobial and well balanced in terms of protein, carbohydrate and fat. Babies tend to love green foods and this purée works perfectly as a dip served with soft cooked vegetables.

Sweet Yoghurt Dip

This easy yoghurt dip is great with diced apples, strawberry, banana, mango, kiwi fruit, pineapple and banana.

Ingredients

- 100g vanilla yoghurt
- 1 tablespoon brown sugar
- 1/8 teaspoon fresh lemon juice
- Pinch of cinnamon

Directions

- In a small bowl, stir together the yoghurt, cinnamon, brown sugar and lemon juice. Refrigerate for at least 30 minutes, then serve with your child's favourite fruits.

Nutrition: It's a good idea to combine protein with fruit in order to help keep blood sugar levels balanced. It is best to use full-fat live yoghurt as this contains beneficial bacteria, which support your baby's digestion and immune system.

Hummus

Great with pitta bread triangles, toast squares, rice crackers or small pretzel sticks.

Ingredients

- 100g canned chickpeas
- 2 tablespoons olive oil
- 1 garlic clove, minced
- ½ teaspoon ground cumin
- ¼ cup tahini (sesame paste)
- Juice of 1 lemon
- Salt to taste
- Pinch of paprika, optional

Directions

- Drain the chickpeas and rinse.
- In a food processor, blend the tahini and lemon juice until smooth. Scrape the mixture from the sides of the food processor. Blend again to produce a smooth purée.
- Add the olive oil, garlic, cumin and salt to the food processor, blend until smooth.
- Finally add the chickpeas and blend till mixture is smooth, adding 1 tablespoon at a time until the desired consistency is achieved.
- Scrape the hummus into a bowl then drizzle about 1 teaspoon of olive oil over the top and sprinkle with paprika, if using.

Nutrition: Hummus is high in fibre and a fantastic source of protein, particularly for vegetarian babies. Chickpeas are one of the best vegetarian sources of iron, which is a key nutrient that babies need plenty of as their stores may become depleted from six months onwards. Hummus also provides calcium for strong bones and is particularly useful if you are avoiding dairy, nuts or gluten.

CONVERSION GUIDE

Oven Temperature Guide

Description	°C (CELCIUS)	°F (FAHRENHEIT)	GAS MARK
Very cool	110	225	
	130	250	
Cool	140	275	1
	150	300	2
Very moderate	170	325	3
Moderate	180	350	4
	190	375	5
Moderately hot	200	400	6
Hot	220	425	7
	230	450	8
Very	240	475	9

Cooking Measurements
Cooking Equivalents

A pinch = ⅛ teaspoon

1 tablespoon = 3 teaspoons

⅛ cup = 2 tablespoons

⅙ cup = 2 tablespoons + 2 teaspoons

¼ cup = 4 tablespoons

⅓ cup = 5 tablespoons + 1 teaspoon

⅜ cup = 6 tablespoons

½ cup = 8 tablespoons

⅔ cup = 10 tablespoons + 2 teaspoons

¾ cup = 12 tablespoons

1 cup = 16 tablespoons

1 cup = 48 teaspoons

1 cup = 8 fluid ounces (fl oz)

2 cups = 1 pint

2 pints = 1 quart

4 cups = 1 quart

4 quarts = 1 gallon (gal)

1 millilitre (ml) = 1 cubic centimetre (cc)

1 inch (in) = 2.54 centimetres (cm)

16 ounces (oz) = 1 pound (lb)

US to Metric System
Converting Fluids

⅕ teaspoon = 1ml

1 teaspoon = 5ml

1 tablespoon = 15ml

1 fluid oz = 30ml

⅕ cup = 50ml

1 cup = 240ml

2 cups (1 pint) = 470ml

4 cups (1 quart) = .95litre

4 quarts (1 gal) = 3.8 litres

Converting Weight

1oz = 28 grams

1 pound = 454 grams

Fluid Measurement Abbreviations
ml means millilitres
cc is the same as ml
oz means ounce (fluid)
gal means gallon

Weight Measurement Abbreviations
g means grams
lbs means pounds
oz means ounces

Weight
1 gram = .035 ounce
100 grams = 3.5 ounces
500 grams = 1.10 pounds
1 kilogram = 2.205 pounds
1 kilogram = 35 oz

Metric System to US
Converting Fluids
1 millilitre = ⅕ teaspoon
5 ml = 1 teaspoon
15 ml = 1 tablespoon
30 ml = 1 fluid oz.
47 ml = ⅕ cup
100 ml = 3.4 fluid oz
237 ml= 1 cup
240 ml = 1 cup
473 ml= 2 cups
.95 litre=4 cups
3.8 litres = 4 quarts (1 gal)
1 litre = 34 fluid oz
1 litre = 4.2 cups
1 litre = 2.1 pints
1 litre = 1.06 quarts
1 litre = .26 gallon

REFERENCES

British Nutrition Foundation 2015, 2015."BNF Factsheet on Weaning your baby."

http://www.nhs.uk/ipgmedia/national/british%20 nutrition%20foundation/assets/weaningyourbaby. pdf

Cichero J.A.Y., 2016. "Introducing solid foods using baby-led weaning vs. spoon-feeding: a focus on oral development, nutrient intake and quality of research to bring balance to the debate." Nutrition Bulletin, 41 1: 72-77.

Gill Rapley, 2008. "Guidelines for implementing a baby-led approach to the introduction of solid foods."

http://www.rapleyweaning.com/assets/blw_ guidelines.pdf

Health Service Executive, 2015. "Feeding your baby: introducing family meals."

https://www.healthpromotion.ie/hp-files/docs/ HPM00971.pdf

NHS UK. "Drinks and cups for babies and toddlers."

http://www.nhs.uk/Conditions/pregnancy-and-baby/ Pages/drinks-and-cups-children.aspx#drinks

NHS UK. "Your Baby's First Solid Foods."

http://www.nhs.uk/Conditions/pregnancy-and-baby/ Pages/solid-foods-weaning.aspx

The Caroline Walker Trust, 2011. "Eating well: first year of life Practical guide."

http://www.cwt.org.uk/wp-content/ uploads/2014/07/CHEW-1stYearLifePracticalGuide. pdf

WORLD HEALTH ORGANIZATION, 2002. "Nutrient Adequacy of Exclusive Breastfeeding for the Term Infant During the First Six Months of Life."

http://apps.who.int/iris/ bitstream/10665/42519/1/9241562110.pdf

WORLD HEALTH ORGANIZATION, 2003. "Guiding principles for complementary feeding of the breastfed child."

http://www.who.int/nutrition/publications/guiding_ principles_compfeeding_breastfed.pdf

WORLD HEALTH ORGANIZATION, 2005. "Guiding Principles for Feeding Non-Breastfed Children 6-24 Months of Age."

http://apps.who.int/iris/ bitstream/10665/43281/1/9241593431. pdf?ua=1&ua=1

INDEX

allergies 22, 46, 51, 89
    allergic reactions 21, 46-7
    low allergenic foods 18
    milk protein allergy 24, 25
    nuts and seeds 88
    premature weaning 12
    see also foods to avoid
apples 17
    Apple and Carrot Purée 64
    Apple and Cinnamon Purée 60-1
    Apple and Cinnamon Yoghurt 94-5
    Apple and Pear Compote 186
    Apple Purée 52
    Apple Strawberry Purée 99
    Apples, Pears and Blueberries 98
    Banana and Apple Purée 56
    Caramelized Peach, Apple, Banana and Shallots 93
    Green Apple Purée 66
    Plumple Purée 60
    Pumpkin and Apple 62-3
    Sweet Potato and Apple 65
Apricot Chicken 116
arsenic 25
aubergines
    Aubergine Sauce 201
    Chicken, Potato and Aubergine Goodness 159
avocados 18
    Avocado, Banana and Kiwi Purée 59
    Avocado and Cucumber Breakfast 97
    Bananacado 98
    Carrot and Avocado Mash 65
    Mashed Avocado 53
baby-led weaning 14-15
Baked Sweet Potatoes 73
bananas 18
    Avocado, Banana and Kiwi Purée 59
    Banana and Apple Purée 56
    Bananacado 98
    Blueberry, Banana and Greek Yoghurt 102
    Blueberry Banana Ice Cream 190-1
    Breakfast Smoothie 180-1
    Caramelized Peach, Apple, Banana and Shallots 93
    Courgette and Banana 63
    Creamy Mango and Banana Purée 57
    Mashed Banana 52
    Mixed Fruit Parfait 192
    Peach and Banana Purée 58
    Strawberry Banana Popsicle 197
    Tropical Fruit Purée 58
Basic Scrambled Eggs 91
beans 89
    Creamy Beans and Vegetable Porridge 148-9
    Green Beans and Pear Purée 66
Béchamel Sauce 158
beef
    Beef and Broccoli Chow Mein 216-17
    Beef Fried Rice 166-7
    Beef with Lentils and Vegetables 168
    Beef Stew 164-5
    Beef Stroganoff 214-15
    Beef with Sweet Potato and Broccoli 120-1
    Kid-friendly Lasagne Bolognese 228-9
    My First Bolognese 128-9
    My First Cottage Pie 119
    Spaghetti and Meatballs 226-7
    Sweet Beef Dinner 119
    Sweet Potato Shepherd's Pie 213-14
beetroot 18
    Beet, Potato and Spinach Purée 107
    Beet Purée 68-9
    Beetroot Chips 242
berries
    Mixed Berry and Pear Compote 61
    see also blueberries; raspberries; strawberries
blueberries
    Apples, Pears and Blueberries 98
    Blueberry, Banana and Greek

Yoghurt 102
Blueberry Banana Ice Cream
190-1
Summer Berry Purée 100-1
Summer Fruit Compote 142-3
bolognese
Kid-friendly Lasagne Bolognese
228-9
My First Bolognese 128-9
Spicy Turkey and Mushroom
Bolognese 204-5
bread 89
French Toast Squares 142
Breakfast Semolina 183
Breakfast Smoothie 180-1
breast milk 12, 17, 19, 24, 43, 50,
137-8
breastfeeding 12, 13
broccoli
Beef and Broccoli Chow Mein
216-17
Beef with Sweet Potato and
Broccoli 120-1
Broccoli and Cauliflower
Gratin 110
Broccoli and Cauliflower Purée
74
Carrot, Broccoli and Butternut
Squash 75
Chicken, Broccoli and
Butternut Squash 117
Coconutty Turkey and Broccoli
163
Creamy Carrot, Broccoli and
Cauliflower Purée 113
Mixed Vegetable in Cheese
Sauce 109

Sweet Potato, Broccoli and
Carrot 71
Yummy Greens Purée 110
brownies
Sweet Potato Brownie 240-1
butternut squash 18
Butternut Squash and Lentils
Goodness 108-9
Butternut Squash and Pear 62
Butternut Squash Purée 54
Carrot, Broccoli and Butternut
Squash 75
Chicken, Broccoli and
Butternut Squash 117
calcium 18, 42
Caramelized Peach, Apple, Banana
and Shallots 93
carbohydrates 39
Carronut Purée 56
carrots 17
Apple and Carrot Purée 64
Carronut Purée 56
Carrot and Avocado Mash 65
Carrot, Broccoli and Butternut
Squash 75
Carrot and Mango Purée 70
Carrot Purée 54
Carrot and Sweet Potato with
Peas 73
Creamy Carrot, Broccoli and
Cauliflower Purée 113
Hidden Carrot Mac and Cheese
170-1
Mixed Vegetable in Cheese
Sauce 109
Parsnip and Carrot Purée 70
Root Vegetable Purée 112-13

Sweet Potato, Broccoli and
Carrot 71
cashew nuts 88
cauliflower
Broccoli and Cauliflower
Gratin 110
Broccoli and Cauliflower Purée
74
Cauliflower Gratin 199
Cauliflower Popcorn 242
Cauliflower and Sweet Potato
Coconut Purée 71
Creamy Carrot, Broccoli and
Cauliflower Purée 113
Creamy Cauliflower and Plaice
125
Creamy Cauliflower and
Potato 105
Leek, Sweet Potato and
Cauliflower 108
Mixed Vegetable in Cheese
Sauce 109
Celery, Leek and Potato Purée 75
cereals 89
Breakfast Semolina 183
Creamy Beans and Vegetable
Porridge 148-9
Fruitilicious Oatmeal 179
Mango Muesli 140-1
Mixed Fruit Porridge 139
Pear Cinnamon Cereal 93
see also rice
cheese 89
Cheesy Potato Bake 144-5
Cheesy Salmon Pasta 172
Cheesy Sole with Sweet
Potatoes 157

Hidden Carrot Mac and Cheese
170-1
Mixed Vegetable in Cheese
Sauce 109
chicken 90
Apricot Chicken 116
Chicken, Broccoli and
Butternut Squash 117
Chicken Egusi Soup 212
Chicken Noodle Soup 203
Chicken, Potato and Aubergine
Goodness 159
Creamy Chicken 117
Fruity Chicken Curry 205
Homemade Chicken Nuggets
202
Kids' Sweet and Sour Chicken
208-9
Micah's Favourite Chicken
Wings 210-11
My First Chicken Purée 115
Nigerian Chicken Stew 206-7
Surf and Turf Fried Rice 220-1
Sweet Chicken Dinner 116-17
Tasty Chicken Couscous 162-3
chips
Beetroot Chips 242
Homemade Sweet Plantain
Chips 238-9
chocolate
Chocolate Dipped Fresh Fruits
188-9
Sweet Potato Brownie 240-1
choking 13, 46, 47, 51, 137, 178
coconut 19
Carronut Purée 56
Cauliflower and Sweet Potato

Coconut Purée 71
Coconutty Turkey and Broccoli
163
Crayfish Tail Coconut Rice 225
Watermelon and Coconut
Popsicle 194-5
cod
Cod Stewed Potatoes 154-5
Cod with Vegetables 124
Mini Fish Pie 158
My First Fish Purée 123
coffee 26
compote
Apple and Pear Compote 186
Mango Compote 60
Mixed Berry and Pear Compote
61
Summer Fruit Compote 142-3
conversion guide 245-7
courgettes
Courgette and Banana 63
Courgette Fries 236-7
Courgette Purée 55
Yummy Greens Purée 110
couscous
Salmon Couscous 224
Tasty Chicken Couscous 162-3
cow's milk 24, 45, 51, 89, 177-8
Crayfish Tail Coconut Rice 225
Creamy Beans and Vegetable
Porridge 148-9
Creamy Carrot, Broccoli and
Cauliflower Purée 113
Creamy Cauliflower and Plaice 125
Creamy Cauliflower and Potato 105
Creamy Chicken 117
Creamy Mango and Banana Purée

57
cucumber
Avocado and Cucumber
Breakfast 97
curry
Fruity Chicken Curry 205
Yummy Oxtail Curry 218-19
dairy produce 89
unpasteurised 25, 46
see also cheese; milk; yoghurt
defrosting food 30-1
dips
Hummus 244
Sweet Yoghurt Dip 243
drinks 24-6, 90, 137-8, 177-8
see also milk
Easy, Yummy Pancakes 182
eggs 89, 137
Basic Scrambled Eggs 91
Easy, Yummy Pancakes 182
Mixed Vegetable Omelette 143
Nigerian Egg Stew 182-3
Plain Omelette 92
Plantain Frittata 184-5
raw eggs 178
egusi
Chicken Egusi Soup 212
equipment
kitchen essentials 29-30
weaning essentials 28-9
fats 40, 177
unsaturated 18
finger foods 14, 15, 22-3, 47, 87-8,
138, 237-44
first foods 17-19
fish 89, 138
Cheesy Sole with Sweet

Potatoes 157
Crayfish Tail Coconut Rice 225
Creamy Cauliflower and Plaice 125
high-mercury fish 46, 178
Homemade Fish Fingers 156
Mini Fish Pie 158
My First Fish Purée 123
Sardine Fusilli 222-3
Surf and Turf Fried Rice 220-1
see also cod; mackerel; salmon
fizzy drinks 26, 90, 178
food poisoning 25, 30, 178
foods to avoid 45-6, 51, 178
see also allergies
formula milk 12, 17, 24, 43, 50, 137-8
non-cow's milk 24
freezing food 30
French Toast Squares 142
frittata
Plantain Frittata 184-5
fruit juices/drinks 25-6, 178
Fruit Salad Purée 143
Fruitilicious Oatmeal 179
Fruity Chicken Curry 205
fussy eating 34-7
Garden Egg Sauce 201
goat's milk 25
gratin
Broccoli and Cauliflower Gratin 110
Cauliflower Gratin 199
Green Apple Purée 66
Green Beans and Pear Purée 66
Green Pea Purée 243

Grilled Pineapple Pops 187
ground nuts 88
health and safety 45-8
Hidden Carrot Mac and Cheese 170-1
Homemade Chicken Nuggets 202
Homemade Fish Fingers 156
Homemade Sweet Plantain Chips 238-9
honey 45, 137
hot drinks 26
Hummus 244
hygiene 48
ice cream
Blueberry Banana Ice Cream 190-1
iron 13, 18, 26, 43, 90
Jollof Risotto 152-3
kale 18-19
Green Apple Purée 66
Kid-friendly Lasagne Bolognese 228-9
Kiddies' Sweetcorn Chowder 146-7
Kids' Sweet and Sour Chicken 208-9
kitchen equipment 29-30
kiwi
Avocado, Banana and Kiwi Purée 59
Chocolate Dipped Fresh Fruits 188-9
Fruit Salad Purée 143
Mixed Fruit Parfait 192
Rainbow Popsicle 196
lactose intolerance 25, 47
Lamb Casserole 169
lauric acid 19
leeks

Celery, Leek and Potato Purée 75
Leek, Sweet Potato and Cauliflower 108
Sweet Potato, Spinach and Leek 111
lentils 89
Beef with Lentils and Vegetables 168
Butternut Squash and Lentils Goodness 108-9
Lentils and Vegetables 106
Macaroni Carbonara 173
mackerel
Ogbono with Mackerel Soup 127
Okra with Mackerel Soup 126
mango
Carrot and Mango Purée 70
Creamy Mango and Banana Purée 57
Mango Compote 60
Mango Muesli 140-1
Mango Purée 53
Mango and Yoghurt Popsicle 193
Rainbow Popsicle 196
Tropical Fruit Purée 58
Marinara Sauce 231
mash
Carrot and Avocado Mash 65
Mashed Avocado 53
Mashed Banana 52
Ripe Plantain Mash 104-5
menu planning 31-2
weekly menu plans 32, 78-85, 130-5, 174-5, 234-5

mercury 46, 178
Micah's Favourite Chicken Wings 210-11
microwaves 31
milk 24, 87, 137-8
    alternatives 25
    cow's milk 24, 45, 51, 89, 177-8
    flavoured milk 26
    goat and sheep's milk 25
    lactose intolerance 25, 47
    milk protein allergy 24, 25
    unpasteurised milk 25, 46
    see also breast milk; formula milk
Mini Fish Pie 158
Mixed Berry and Pear Compote 61
Mixed Fruit Parfait 192
Mixed Fruit Porridge 139
Mixed Vegetable in Cheese Sauce 109
Mixed Vegetable Medley 72
Mixed Vegetable Omelette 143
muesli
    Mango Muesli 140-1
mushroom
    Mushroom Ratatouille 200
    Spicy Turkey and Mushroom Bolognese 204-5
My First Bolognese 128-9
My First Chicken Purée 115
My First Cottage Pie 119
My First Fish Purée 123
My First Okra Soup 76-7
Nigerian Chicken Stew 206-7
Nigerian Egg Stew 182-3
noodles

Beef and Broccoli Chow Mein 216-17
    Chicken Noodle Soup 203
nuts and nut products 88, 178
oatmeal
    Fruitilicious Oatmeal 179
    see also porridge
Ogbono with Mackerel Soup 127
okra 138
    My First Okra Soup 76-7
    Okra with Mackerel Soup 126
    Okra with Mixed Vegetables 150
omelette
    Mixed Vegetable Omelette 143
    Plain Omelette 92
oxtail
    Yummy Oxtail Curry 218-19
pancakes
    Easy, Yummy Pancakes 182
papaya
    Papaya Purée 53
    Tropical Fruit Purée 58
parsnips 18
    Parsnip and Carrot Purée 70
    Parsnip Purée 55
    Root Vegetable Purée 112-13
    Watercress, Potato and Parsnip 114
pasta 89
    Cheesy Salmon Pasta 172
    Hidden Carrot Mac and Cheese 170-1
    Kid-friendly Lasagne Bolognese 228-9
    Macaroni Carbonara 173
    Pasta with Hidden Vegetable

Sauce 230
    Penne with Vegetables 232-3
    Salmon Pasta 129
    Sardine Fusilli 222-3
    Spaghetti and Meatballs 226-7
peaches
    Caramelized Peach, Apple, Banana and Shallots 93
    Peach and Banana Purée 58
    Peachy Yoghurt 102
peanuts 178
pears 17
    Apple and Pear Compote 186
    Apples, Pears and Blueberries 98
    Butternut Squash and Pear 62
    Chocolate Dipped Fresh Fruits 188-9
    Green Beans and Pear Purée 66
    Mixed Berry and Pear Compote 61
    Pear Cinnamon Cereal 93
    Pear and Prunes 61
    Pear Purée 52
    Pear and Raspberry 99
    Sweet Pea Purée 67
peas
    Carrot and Sweet Potato with Peas 73
    Green Pea Purée 243
    Mixed Vegetable in Cheese Sauce 109
    Sweet Pea Purée 67
    Yummy Greens Purée 110
Penne with Vegetables 232-3
pies

Mini Fish Pie 158
My First Cottage Pie 119
Sweet Potato Shepherd's Pie
    213-14
pineapple
    Fruit Salad Purée 143
    Grilled Pineapple Pops 187
plaice
    Creamy Cauliflower and Plaice
    125
Plain Omelette 92
plantain
    Homemade Sweet Plantain
    Chips 238-9
    Plantain Frittata 184-5
    Plantain Pottage 151
    Ripe Plantain Mash 104-5
Plumple Purée 60
popsicles
    Mango and Yoghurt Popsicle
    193
    Rainbow Popsicle 196
    Strawberry Banana Popsicle
    197
    Watermelon and Coconut
    Popsicle 194-5
pork
    Sweet Pork Dinner 167
porridge
    Creamy Beans and Vegetable
    Porridge 148-9
    Mixed Fruit Porridge 139
    Rice Porridge 103
potatoes
    Beet, Potato and Spinach
    Purée 107
    Celery, Leek and Potato Purée
    75
    Cheesy Potato Bake 144-5
    Chicken, Potato and Aubergine
    Goodness 159
    Cod Stewed Potatoes 154-5
    Creamy Cauliflower and
    Potato 105
    Potato Pottage 198-9
    Ratatouille Baked Potatoes
    150-1
    Root Vegetable Purée 112-13
    Watercress, Potato and Parsnip
    114
pottage
    Plantain Pottage 151
    Potato Pottage 198-9
prawns
    Surf and Turf Fried Rice 220-1
protein 40, 89, 90
prunes
    Pear and Prunes 61
pulses 89
    see also lentils
Pumpkin and Apple 62-3
purées
    Apple and Carrot Purée 64
    Apple and Cinnamon Purée
    60-1
    Apple Purée 52
    Apple Strawberry Purée 99
    Avocado, Banana and Kiwi
    Purée 59
    Banana and Apple Purée 56
    Beet, Potato and Spinach
    Purée 107
    Beet Purée 68-9
    Broccoli and Cauliflower Purée
    74
    Butternut Squash Purée 54
    Carronut Purée 56
    Carrot and Mango Purée 70
    Carrot Purée 54
    Cauliflower and Sweet Potato
    Coconut Purée 71
    Celery, Leek and Potato Purée
    75
    Courgette Purée 55
    Creamy Carrot, Broccoli and
    Cauliflower Purée 113
    Creamy Mango and Banana
    Purée 57
    Fruit Salad Purée 143
    Green Apple Purée 66
    Green Beans and Pear Purée
    66
    Green Pea Purée 243
    Mango Purée 53
    My First Chicken Purée 115
    My First Fish Purée 123
    Papaya Purée 53
    Parsnip and Carrot Purée 70
    Parsnip Purée 55
    Peach and Banana Purée 58
    Pear Purée 52
    Plumple Purée 60
    Root Vegetable Purée 112-13
    Summer Berry Purée 100-1
    Sweet Pea Purée 67
    Sweet Potato Purée 54
    Tasty Turkey Purée 118
    Tropical Fruit Purée 58
    Yummy Greens Purée 110
Rainbow Popsicle 196
raspberries

Pear and Raspberry 99
Summer Berry Purée 100-1
Summer Fruit Compote 142-3
Ratatouille 112
Mushroom Ratatouille 200
Ratatouille Baked Potatoes 150-1
reheating food 31
rice
Beef Fried Rice 166-7
Crayfish Tail Coconut Rice 225
drinks 25
Jollof Risotto 152-3
Rice Porridge 103
Surf and Turf Fried Rice 220-1
Ripe Plantain Mash 104-5
Root Vegetable Purée 112-13
salmon 138
Cheesy Salmon Pasta 172
Salmon Couscous 224
Salmon Pasta 129
Salmon with Potato and Broccoli 125
salmonella 178
salt 45, 89, 137
Sardine Fusilli 222-3
sauces
Aubergine Sauce 201
Béchamel Sauce 158
Garden Egg Sauce 201
Marinara Sauce 231
Mixed Vegetable in Cheese Sauce 109
Pasta with Hidden Vegetable Sauce 230
seeds 88
self-feeding 22-4

semolina
Breakfast Semolina 183
shallots
Caramelized Peach, Apple, Banana and Shallots 93
sheep's milk 25
Simple African Vegetable Soup 160-1
Simple Minestrone 144
smoothies 25-6
Breakfast Smoothie 180-1
snacks 177
sole
Cheesy Sole with Sweet Potatoes 157
soup
Chicken Egusi Soup 212
Chicken Noodle Soup 203
Kiddies' Sweetcorn Chowder 146-7
My First Okra Soup 76-7
Ogbono with Mackerel Soup 127
Okra with Mackerel Soup 126
Simple African Vegetable Soup 160-1
Simple Minestrone 144
soya drinks 24, 25
Spaghetti and Meatballs 226-7
spinach
Beet, Potato and Spinach Purée 107
Simple African Vegetable Soup 160-1
Sweet Potato, Spinach and Leek 111
spoon-led weaning 15

stew
Beef Stew 164-5
Cod Stewed Potatoes 154-5
Nigerian Chicken Stew 206-7
Nigerian Egg Stew 182-3
store-bought food 21-2, 30, 48
storing food 30
strawberries
Apple Strawberry Purée 99
Breakfast Smoothie 180-1
Chocolate Dipped Fresh Fruits 188-9
Fruit Salad Purée 143
Mixed Fruit Parfait 192
Rainbow Popsicle 196
Strawberry Banana Popsicle 197
Summer Berry Purée 100-1
Summer Fruit Compote 142-3
sugar 46, 137, 177
Summer Berry Purée 100-1
Summer Fruit Compote 142-3
Surf and Turf Fried Rice 220-1
Sweet Beef Dinner 119
Sweet Chicken Dinner 116-17
Sweet Pea Purée 67
Sweet Pork Dinner 167
sweet potatoes 18
Baked Sweet Potatoes 73
Beef with Sweet Potato and Broccoli 120-1
Carrot and Sweet Potato with Peas 73
Cauliflower and Sweet Potato Coconut Purée 71
Cheesy Sole with Sweet Potatoes 157

Leek, Sweet Potato and
        Cauliflower 108
Sweet Potato and Apple 65
Sweet Potato, Broccoli and
        Carrot 71
Sweet Potato Brownie 240-1
Sweet Potato Purée 54
Sweet Potato Shepherd's Pie
        213-14
Sweet Potato, Spinach and
        Leek 111
Sweet Yoghurt Dip 243
sweetcorn
        Kiddies' Sweetcorn Chowder
        146-7
Tasty Chicken Couscous 162-3
Tasty Turkey Purée 118
tea 26
thawing frozen food 30-1
tooth decay 25, 26, 177, 178
treats 177
Tropical Fruit Purée 58
turkey 90
        Coconutty Turkey and Broccoli
        163
        Spicy Turkey and Mushroom
        Bolognese 204-5
        Tasty Turkey Purée 118
unpasteurised dairy products 25, 46
Vanilla Custard 96-7
Veal with Vegetables 122
vitamins and minerals 17, 18, 41-3,
        51, 178
water 24-5, 90
Watercress, Potato and Parsnip 114
Watermelon and Coconut Popsicle
        194-5

weaning
        essential equipment 28-9
        first foods 17-19
        homemade vs. store bought
                food 21-2
        methods 14-15
        self-feeding 22-4
        stages 16
        starting solids 13-14
        strategies 19-21
weekly menu plans 32, 78-85, 130-
        5, 174-5, 234-5
yoghurt
        Apple and Cinnamon Yoghurt
                94-5
        Blueberry, Banana and Greek
                Yoghurt 102
        Breakfast Smoothie 180-1
        Mango and Yoghurt Popsicle
                193
        Mixed Fruit Parfait 192
        Peachy Yoghurt 102
        Sweet Yoghurt Dip 243
Yummy Greens Purée 110
Yummy Oxtail Curry 218-19